Shire County Guide 12

BEDFORDSHIRE

James Dyer

Shire Publications Ltd

Published in 1995 by Shire Publications Ltd, Cromwell House, Church Street, Princes Risborough, Buckinghamshire HP27 9AA, UK.
Copyright © 1987 and 1995 by James Dyer. First published 1987. Enlarged second edition 1995. Shire County Guide 12. ISBN 0 7478 0269 6.

Printed in Great Britain by CIT Printing Services, Press Buildings, Merlins Bridge, Haverfordwest, Dyfed SA61 1XF.

British Library Cataloguing in Publication Data
Dyer, James
Bedfordshire. – 2Rev.ed. – (Shire County Guides; No. 12)
I. Title II. Series
914.25604859
ISBN 0-7478-0269-6

Acknowledgements

The author wishes to thank the following for their assistance: David Baker, Peggy Baldwin, Harry Barr, Marina Brown, Betty Chambers, Keith Robinson, Jean Sewell and Bernard B. West. Special thanks go to Dr Nancy Dawson for assistance with chapter 3.

Photographs are acknowledged to: Anderson Photography, Leighton Buzzard, page 107; Cecil Higgins Art Gallery and Museum, page 94; *Illustrated London News*, page 26; Cadbury Lamb, pages 96 and 99; Philip Salter, page 47; Shuttleworth Collection, page 95; Persis Tallents, page 104; Wernher Collection, page 86. All other photographs including the cover are by the author. The map on page 5 is by Robert Dizon.

Ordnance Survey grid references

National Grid References are included for many of the places described in this book, particularly for the harder-to-find places in chapters 3 and 4, for the benefit of those readers who have the Ordnance Survey 1:50,000 Landranger maps of the area. The references are stated as a Landranger sheet number followed by the 100 km National Grid square and the six-figure reference.

To locate a site by means of the grid reference, proceed as in the following example: Conger Hill (OS 166: TL 011289). Take the OS Landranger map sheet 166 ('Luton, Hertford and District'). The grid numbers are printed in blue around the edges of the map. In more recently produced maps these numbers are repeated at 10 km intervals throughout the map, so that it is not necessary to open it out completely.) Read off these numbers from the left along the top edge of the map until you come to 01, denoting a vertical grid line, then estimate one-tenth of the distance to vertical line 02 and envisage an imaginary vertical grid line 01.1 at this point. Next look at the grid numbers at one side of the map (either side will do) and read *upwards* until you find the horizontal grid line 28. Estimate nine-tenths of the distance to the next horizontal line above (i.e. 29), and so envisage an imaginary horizontal line across the map at 28.9. Follow this imaginary line across the map until it crosses the imaginary vertical line 01.1. At the intersection of these two lines you will find Conger Hill.

The Ordnance Survey Landranger maps which cover Bedfordshire are sheets 153, 165 and 166. Very small areas of the county are found on map 152.

Cover: *Clophill Green, with the Green Man and High Street.*

Contents

Preface

Welcome to the Shire County Guide to Bedfordshire, one of over thirty such books, written and designed to enable you to organise your time in the county well.

The Shire County Guides fill the need for a compact, accurate and thorough guide to each county so that visitors can plan a half-day excursion or a whole week's stay to best advantage. Residents, too, will find the guides a handy and reliable reference to the places of interest in their area.

Travelling British roads can be time consuming, and the County Guides will ensure that you need not inadvertently miss any interesting feature in a locality, that you do not accidentally bypass a new museum or an outstanding church, that you can find an attractive place to picnic, and that you will appreciate the history and the buildings of the towns or villages in which you stop.

This book has been arranged in special interest chapters, such as the countryside, historic buildings or archaeology, and all these places of interest are located on the map on page 5. Use the map either for an overview to decide which area has most to interest you, or to help you enjoy your immediate neighbourhood. Then refer to the nearest town or village in chapter 2 to see, at a glance, what special features or attractions each community contains or is near. The subsequent chapters enable readers with a particular interest to find immediately those places of importance to them, while the cross-referencing under 'Towns and villages' assists readers with wider tastes to select how best to spend their time.

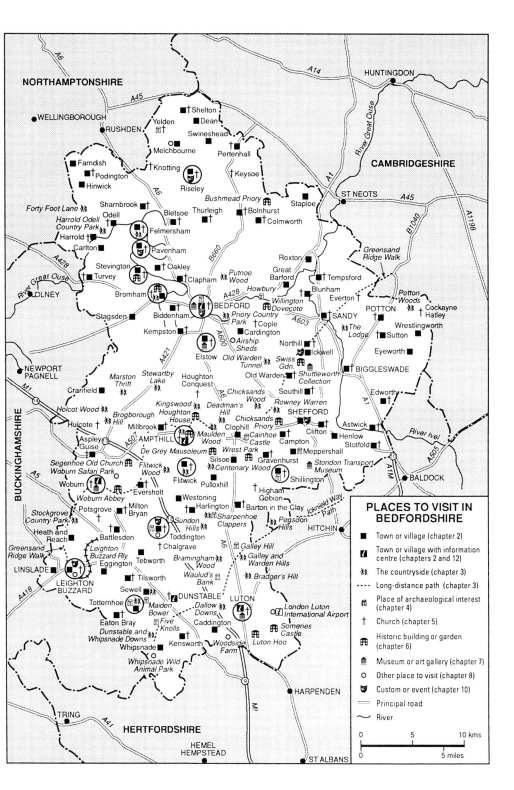

NORTHAMPTONSHIRE

● WELLINGBOROUGH

● RUSHDEN

■† Shelton
Yelden ■ Dean
Swineshead ■

○ Melchbourne
Pertenhall †

■ Farndish
■† Podington
■ Hinwick
†Knotting
† Keysoe

Riseley

CAMBRIDGESHIRE

ST NEOTS ● A45

Bushmead Priory

Forty Foot Lane 杰 Sharnbrook ■†
Harrold Odell Odell
Country Park ■†
Harrold †
Carlton ■

Bletsoe † Thurleigh †Bolnhurst
Felmersham
Pavenham
†Colmworth

Staploe ■

Roxton ■

Greensand Ridge Walk

Stevington ■
■† Turvey

†Oakley
Clapham †

Putnoe Wood

Great Barford

†Tempsford ■

Blunham
Everton †

Potton Woods

OLNEY ●

Bromham

Howbury
A428

BEDFORD

A428

Willington Dovecote
Priory Country Park

A603

SANDY

POTTON 杰 ● Cockayne
Hatley

The Lodge 杰
†Sutton

Wrestlingworth ■

Stagsden ■

Biddenham

Kempston ■†

†Cople
Cardington ■

○ Airship Sheds

Elstow

Old Warden Tunnel

Northill ■
Ickwell ■

Eyeworth ■

Swiss Gdn.
Shuttleworth † Collection

BIGGLESWADE ■

NEWPORT PAGNELL ●

Marston Thrift

Stewartby Lake 杰

Houghton Conquest †

Old Warden ■

M1

Cranfield ■

Holcot Wood 杰

Hulcote †

Brogborough
Houghton Hill 杰 House

Millbrook ■†

Chicksands Wood

Kingswood 杰 Deadman's
Hill 杰

Southill †

Rowney Warren

SHEFFORD ■

Edworth ■

Astwick ■

Aspley
Guise ⑫

AMPTHILL ⑫

Maulden
Wood

Clophill †
Chicksands
Priory

Cainhoe
Castle

Clifton †
Campton ■

Henlow
Stotfold ■

River Ivel

Segenhoe Old Church ⊞
Woburn Safari Park ○

De Grey Mausoleum ⊞

Silsoe ■

Wrest Park ⊞

Meppershall †

BALDOCK ●

Flitwick
Wood 杰

杰 Centenary Wood

Gravenhurst ■†

Stondon Transport Museum 血

A1M

Wobum ■

Woburn Abbey ⊞

Flitwick ■
Pulloxhill ■

Shillington †

Stockgrove Country Park 杰

Eversholt †

Potsgrove † Milton
Bryan ■†

Higham Gobion †

Westoning ■

Harlington †

Barton in the Clay ■†

Icknield Way Path

Heath and
Reach ■

Battlesden ■

Sundon
Hills 杰

杰Sharpenhoe
Clappers

Pegsdon
Hills 杰

HITCHIN ●

Greensand
Ridge Walk 杰

Leighton
Buzzard Rly.
Eggington ■

Tebworth ■

Toddington ⑫

†Chalgrave

Galley Hill ⊞

Bramingham 杰
Wood

杰 Galley and
Warden Hills

LINSLADE ●

Tilsworth ■

Waulud's
Bank 杰

杰 Bradger's Hill

LEIGHTON
BUZZARD

Sewell ■

Totternhoe ⊞杰

Maiden
Bower

DUNSTABLE ⑫

LUTON ⑫

London Luton
International Airport ○⑰

Eaton Bray ■†

Five
Knolls

Dallow
Downs 杰

Someries
Castle ⊞

Dunstable and 杰
Whipsnade Downs

Caddington ■

Kensworth ■

Woodside
Farm ○

Luton Hoo ⊞

Whipsnade ■

Whipsnade Wild
Animal Park ○

HARPENDEN ●

**PLACES TO VISIT IN
BEDFORDSHIRE**

■ Town or village (chapter 2)

⑫ Town or village with information
centre (chapters 2 and 12)

杰 The countryside (chapter 3)

---- Long-distance path (chapter 3)

⊞ Place of archaeological interest
(chapter 4)

† Church (chapter 5)

⊞ Historic building or garden
(chapter 6)

血 Museum or art gallery (chapter 7)

○ Other place to visit (chapter 8)

⑰ Custom or event (chapter 10)

═ Principal road

∿ River

HERTFORDSHIRE

● TRING

HEMEL
HEMPSTEAD ●

ST ALBANS ●

0		5		10 kms

0			5 miles

1
This is Bedfordshire

Bedfordshire is a secret, unobtrusive county. High-speed trains and motorways pass through it, and travellers leave Luton Airport from it, but few people ever stop and enjoy this small area, which is neither the Midlands, East Anglia nor the Home Counties. The Chiltern Hills run across its southern limit to provide magnificent scenery, and the Great Ouse flows through the centre amongst undulating meadows and woodland. Imposed on to this background are the great residential and industrial areas of the Luton-Dunstable conurbation and Bedford-Kempston.

Although there are splendid wide viewpoints like Millbrook, Shillington or Sandy, it is perhaps more accurate to write of Bedfordshire in terms of cameos: the close-up view in which the visitor looks at selected points in detail. In this book the author has chosen innumerable cameos and tried to draw attention to them. More than one hundred villages and towns are described, each because it has something special to offer the visitor. In compiling this guide, the writer visited every village and church in the county. He found eighty per cent of the churches locked, a sad reflection on the present state of society. He also found that forty per cent of the churches carried no notice telling where a key might be obtained, a sad reflection on the care of the clergy, and a discourtesy to those who have travelled far to enjoy them.

Bedfordshire is very much a divided county. North and south seldom mix. For the inhabitants of Luton and Dunstable the county seems to end around Barton or Toddington. For Bedford it stretches as far south as Ampthill. Leighton Buzzard and Biggleswade have their own catchment areas. The divide has been emphasised by politics, not only at national level with political divisions between north and south, but at a local level. There is no love lost between Bedford and Luton. In 1964 Luton became a County Borough, responsible for its own affairs; ten years later it

lost its status and fell once more under the yoke of Bedford. Yet there are similarities between the two towns that could help to unite them, particularly the multi-ethnic societies which are so strong in both, and the emphasis on engineering and education which both enjoy. Bedford has public schools and both Luton and Bedford have universities created in 1993 and 1994 respectively.

Bedfordshire is essentially an agricultural county, most of it given over to arable farming, but with the emphasis on market gardening in the east around Biggleswade, 'where the Brussels sprouts grow green'. Its raw materials are clay, sand and chalk, and these have been quarried in vast areas, especially at Marston Moretaine, Leighton Buzzard and Kensworth. Light engineering is found in all towns and most villages, but the heavier motor-car and truck manufacturing industry is largely confined to Luton and Leighton Buzzard. Agricultural and aeronautical research figures prominently in the county at Silsoe, Old Warden, Thurleigh and Cranfield.

Britain's first motorway, the M1, cuts through the west of the county and the realigned A1 runs along the eastern boundary. Two main-line railways run north–south. Only east to west travel is difficult and plans to improve facilities have been mooted for years. Luton's international airport has made it world-famous, yet for millions who pass through that is the only corner of the county they see, and few of them could identify the county's name.

For the visitor to Bedfordshire the advice is simple: get away from the motorways on to the country roads. The towns are interesting, but the villages are full of surprises. Explore them in spring before the leaves on the trees obscure the views, or in autumn when those same trees provide palettes of rich autumn colours. Bedfordshire is a secret county waiting to be discovered.

Pillow lacemaking

The pillow-lace industry developed in the East Midlands in the second half of the sixteenth century. In Bedfordshire it centred on Cranfield and spread along the Ouse valley between Harrold and Eaton Socon. It was probably introduced by refugees from religious persecution in the Netherlands and France between 1550 and 1575. One of the earliest references, dated 1596, relates to Eaton Socon (now in Cambridgeshire), where a woman was paid 2d a week to teach children to work bone (pillow) lace. The trade was practised by both men and women. At first the lace was peddled from door to door, but by the seventeenth century organised lace buyers were visiting the Ouse valley villages and then retailing their produce in London. The industry declined steadily in the nineteenth century because of competition from the plait industry, the inability to compete with continental lace and the growth of machine lace production.

Bedfordshire lace is distinguished by having its pattern and background worked together in a single process, unlike the rival lace industry of Honiton in Devon, where the pattern was worked separately and then joined with a mesh background. Pillow lace and its manufacture are displayed in the Bedford and Luton museums. Demonstrations of pillow lacemaking are given at Stockwood Craft Museum, Luton, during the summer.

Straw plait and the hat industry

Late sixteenth-century religious refugees from the Netherlands probably introduced the straw-plait industry to Bedfordshire. Plaiting of local straw, which could then be sewn into hats, was a cottage industry in almost every village, learnt by boys and girls from youngest childhood. They were taught in plaiting schools, often in squalid conditions: a room 10 feet (3 metres) square for forty children is on record. The finished plait was sold to dealers who travelled around the villages or bought it at plait markets in towns like Luton, Dunstable, Toddington, Ampthill or Shefford. Luton had two large plait market halls opened in 1868 but now destroyed. The import of cheap plait from the Far East brought the decline of the local plait industry in the last quarter of the nineteenth century.

Fourteen thousand people depended upon the manufacture of straw hats in south Bedfordshire in 1689. At first all production was in the home or local sewing room. In Dunstable small factories developed, dominating the trade, its position on the busy Watling Street providing excellent opportunities for selling to travellers. Later, rapid growth of domestic workshops, followed by the arrival of the railway, allowed Luton to take precedence, and Dunstable's trade declined. The energy of the brothers Edmund and Thomas Waller of Luton fostered the rapid growth of the industry through the southeast Midlands. By the mid nineteenth century factories were established in Luton and Dunstable, some employing as many as five hundred hat sewers. Machine stitching and blocking of hats revolutionised the industry, and straw hats continued to be popular until the 1930s, when there was a massive decline from which the industry has never fully recovered. Felt hatmaking was introduced to Luton in the 1870s but did not make much impact until after the First World War. By 1939 felt hats accounted for three-quarters of the hat industry. Following a long period during which hats were not particularly popular, the shrunken industry is now facing a long overdue revival.

Luton Museum houses exhibits illustrating the history of the industry.

2
Towns and villages

Ampthill

Early closing Tuesday.

Small, concise and full of interest, Ampthill's attractions start at the crossroads with the obelisk pump (1784) and the Moot Hall, with clock and cupola, rebuilt in 1852. Also in the market square is a Georgian shop with a wooden arcaded front that was formerly the plait market. Beyond in Church Street are Avenue House and other fine buildings. Number 28 has gates reputedly from Ampthill Great Park. Opposite, number 31 is of Tudor date. Dynevor House (1725) and Brandreth House (about 1814) face each other across Church Square, dwarfing the Feoffee Almshouses (a feoffee was a trustee), parts of which are more than four hundred years old. A public footpath from the King's Arms Yard runs beside a splendid private garden which is well worth diverting to see. In Dunstable Street the White Hart is an early eighteenth-century coaching inn. Close by, the early Georgian brick gazebo, now housing a gold-smith's shop, is unusual. Woburn Street includes the thatched Ossory *cottages ornées* built in 1812, 1815 and 1816. Opposite is the glorious Alameda (Spanish for a public walk), an avenue of lime trees 640 metres (700 yards) long, given to the town by Lord and Lady Holland in 1827. A climb up Park Hill and down Brewery Lane reveals interesting ver-nacular buildings. West of the A507 near Littlepark Farm are the John Cross Almshouses of the late seventeenth century.

Ampthill Park, page 47; Avenue House, page 82; church of St Andrew, page 63; Cooper's Hill, page 50; Houghton House, page 83.

In the locality: the de Grey Mausoleum, page 83; Segenhoe Old Church, page 86; and churches at Flitwick, page 69; and Millbrook, page 74.

Aspley Guise

Praised for its dry warm climate and de-scribed as an 'inland Bournemouth', the vil-lage attracted many middle-class Victorians, and it is their houses which form the majority of older buildings in the village today. The Old House in a lane off High Street was built by Edmund Harding about 1575. It is timber-framed with brick infilling and was restored in the eighteenth century and 1921. Undoubt-edly the finest house in the village is Aspley House, built in 1695, perhaps by an assistant of Wren. The garden façade is about fifty years later. Good views can be obtained from East Street and through the gate in High Street. Guise House, built early in the eighteenth century, was once the Classical Academy, a flourishing progressive school that had more than two hundred boys on its register. It closed in 1845. Away from the village centre are old buildings around the Wheatsheaf in New Town.

Aspley Heath is famous for the fuller's earth quarried there. The village is mainly a street of Victorian and later houses, stretch-ing westwards on to Wavendon Heath, where there are delightful walks. Edgbury, Homewood and Daneswood are all convales-cent homes, recalling James Williamson's 1856 comments on the local climate. St Michael's church was designed by Clutton in 1868 with later additions by Blomfield (1889). For addicts of Victorian architecture it is a gem. Fifty-seven years earlier is Humphry Repton's Henry VII Lodge beside the A5130, just south of the Woburn Sands main cross-roads. There he attempted to produce a per-fect Tudor house by copying parts of known historical buildings.

Church of St Botolph, page 63.

Aspley Heath

See under Aspley Guise, above.

Astwick

This is one of the county's smallest parishes. There are two farmhouses, Church Farm with a five-hundred-year-old mulberry tree, and

Church Street, Ampthill. Avenue House is in the centre.

Bury Farm with a well-preserved moat around it. In the south is a disused watermill with one of the largest wheels in the county.
Church of St Guthlac, page 63.

Barton in the Clay

The name of the village means 'the barley farm in clay land', but there is no historical continuity for the spurious modern use of the name 'Barton-le-Clay'. The name has also acquired a new twentieth-century use: to 'bartonise' a village means to permit uncontrolled planning totally out of scale and keeping with the locality and existing buildings. This is Barton's tragedy and the development on the north side of the village is deplorable, but there is also a good side. In Manor Road (formerly Rogues Lane) is the manor house of the Willes family. The lane beside St Nicholas's church makes an attractive introduction to the hills beyond. The Rectory dates at least to the sixteenth century and is moated. There are good brick and timber-framed cottages here, some with thatch. South of the village are the rounded Barton Hills – The Steps, Flagstaff, Bonfire Knoll and Plum Pudden. At the foot of the hills are springs, a popular spot for visitors, and once famous for

their watercress. North of the present village is the moated site of Faldo Manor, with a deserted medieval village close by.
Church of St Nicholas, page 63.

Battlesden

Battlesden is a tiny hamlet of four red-brick houses, built for the Duke of Bedford in 1887, and two farms. The nineteenth-century manor house was pulled down after little more than twenty years, and today only the stable block remains as Battlesden House. The grounds were laid out by Joseph Paxton in 1821 and still survive. The delightful church of St Peter is in Battlesden Park.
Church of St Peter, page 63.

Bedford

Early closing Thursday; market day Saturday.

Bedford's greatest asset is the river Ouse with its fine tree-lined frontage. The town began in Saxon times and by 886 was on the boundary between the Danes and the kingdom of Alfred. Edward the Elder ordered the extension of the settlement south of the river in 915. After the Norman conquest a wooden motte and bailey castle was constructed, and in 1087

St Paul's spire rises above the Swan Hotel at Bedford.

this belonged to Hugh de Beauchamp, who almost certainly began to rebuild it in stone. A siege took place in 1224 after Falkes de Breauté had seized the castle; afterwards eighty men were hanged from the battlements and the building was dismantled. By the twelfth century Bedford had a stone bridge over the river, on which stood a chapel. In 1566 Sir William Harpur and his wife Dame Alice endowed a school in the town: as a result four schools are administered today in Bedford by the Harpur Trust. In the seventeenth century the town began to develop its river trade. This was interrupted by the Civil War, in which the county nominally supported Parliament, though it is more correct to consider it neutral. With the Restoration Bedford became a centre of religious conflict. Numerous local dissenters were jailed, the most famous being John Bunyan, whose statue by J. E. Boehm (1874) stands at the corner of St Peter's Green. Nineteenth-century development was at first slow, but with the coming of the railways industry began to expand, at first specialising in agricultural equipment. By the 1880s there was a population boom, mainly of the middle classes, which may be explained

by the snobbish popularity of Bedford's schools. It became a university town in 1994.

Today Bedford is a cosmopolitan town with more than seventy nationalities. Less than half the size of Luton in the south, it has suffered the same fate of losing much of its individuality. More of its finer buildings remain, but they are swamped by the offices of multinational companies that dominate the town. Insurance companies and building societies proliferate, and the shopping centre repeats the range of stores found throughout Britain and much of western Europe.

The visitor might begin his tour at St Paul's church. Opposite the church are the old Town Hall, which was once the Harpur schoolhouse (1767), and the red-brick Shire Hall designed by 'Prudential' Waterhouse in 1879-81. Pass John Howard's statue by Alfred Gilbert (1894) and the Swan Hotel by the river. It was designed by Henry Holland and contains a seventeenth-century staircase from Houghton House. Crossing the bridge designed by the local architect John Wing in 1813, walk to the late seventeenth-century College House and St Mary's church. Further south is St John's Hospital, a twelfth-century stone building with considerable later medieval work surviving. It is believed that here John Bunyan was converted to Independency by John Gilford, the rector, who was probably the model for the Interpreter in *The Pilgrim's Progress*. St John's church was drastically restored in 1869-70. Founded in 1180 as the private chapel of St John's Hospital, it is aisleless and has a fourteenth-century piscina and sedilia. The west tower is fifteenth-century. Notice St Mary's House in St Mary's Square, on the opposite side of the road, and then return to the river by Chethams.

After crossing the Suspension Bridge (1888), walk through the riverside gardens to Newnham Road. The castle mound, Cecil Higgins Art Gallery and Bedford Museum are all together here and deserve long visits. At the eastern end of Mill Lane is the house where John Howard, the prison reformer and High Sheriff of Bedfordshire, lived from 1765 to 1789. Beside it is the Bunyan Meeting of 1849, with pictorial bronze doors by Frederick Thrupp. Its museum is open on summer afternoons. Proceed along St Cuthbert's Street and reach the Merton Centre, a sensitive modern development which turns into St Peter's Street, where the church of St Peter de Merton can be found. Bunyan's statue stands at the crossroads, and running north is De Parys Avenue, the town's most attractive tree-lined road away from the river, leading to Bedford Park (where there is a restaurant).

West of the statue is Dame Alice Street with its row of neo-Tudor almshouses with steep dormer windows of 1801 and 1890, and beyond is Bedford Prison (1801) with its carefully detailed pediments and fenestration, hiding many unhappy secrets. Lovers of architecture will enjoy Adelaide Square and The Crescent.

Return to Harpur Street, where the old Modern School frontage by Edward Blore (1830) has been retained to hide the Harpur Shopping Centre. Opposite is the Harpur Suite of 1834 and the not unpleasant glass and concrete Public Library (1972). The Salvation Army Citadel in Commercial Road is one of the most attractive new buildings in the town, and beyond it to the south across the river is County Hall (1969), attractively land-scaped amongst water and trees.

To the east, the village of **Goldington** has now become part of Bedford. Its fine green still survives beside the busy A428. Seventeenth-century Goldington Hall, where Edward Fitzgerald once stayed, is now a hotel. Horse-chestnuts line the busy road to St Mary's church with its fifteenth-century tower and chancel. It was neatly enlarged in 1955-6. Neolithic henge monuments were excavated here in 1987 on the Tesco supermarket site.

Bedford Castle, page 59; **Bedford Museum**, page 93; **Bedford Regatta**, page 106; **Bedford River Festival**, page 106; **Bunyan Meeting Museum and Library**, page 93; **Cecil Higgins Art Gallery and Museum**, page 93; **church of St Mary**, page 63; **church of St Paul**, page 64; **church of St Peter de Merton**, page 64; **Priory Country Park**, page 56; **Putnoe Wood**, page 56; **St Mary's Church Archaeology Centre**, page 93.

In the locality: Airship Sheds, page 97; Bromham Mill, page 82; Elstow Moot Hall, page 93; Stevington Post Mill, page 87; Willington Dovecote and Stables, page 88; and churches at Biddenham, page 64; Bromham, page 65; Clapham, page 66; Cople, page 67; Elstow, page 68; Houghton Conquest, page 70; Kempston, page 71; Oakley, page 75; and Stevington, page 78.

Biddenham

This lovely village lies in a loop of the Ouse, where, in the nineteenth century, for the first time in the English river gravels, James Wyatt found palaeolithic stone implements together with the bones of extinct animals. There is new housing, but the old spreads along the main street with plenty of trees and broad green verges on either side. Buildings in local stone or ochre colour-washed plaster with thatch make it hard to believe that Bedford is only a mile away. There are pleasant walks from the church down to the river Ouse.

Church of St James, page 64.

Biggleswade

Early closing Thursday; market day Saturday.

The large market square is full of potential but is in urgent need of some enlightened

The former Sun Inn at Biggleswade, now private houses.

planning to revitalise it. Nevertheless, there is much in Biggleswade to enjoy. St Andrew's church and the timber-framed buildings close to it form one of the most interesting groups in the town.

The Great North Road originally ran through the town and many coaches stopped there. Numerous inns catered for the traveller including the Swan, the Crown, the Oak and the Rose. The oldest, still surviving, is the White Hart, while the Sun, which was considered one of the best inns in England by John Byng, who stayed there many times in the 1780s, has been restored as a block of houses in Sun Street.

The town's history is a long one. Aerial photographs revealed a Roman camp on Furzehall Common and a late Norman castle between the Ivel and the A1, west of St Andrew's church. There is evidence to suggest that the town was deliberately 'planted' at the beginning of the thirteenth century, although there was already a river bridge at the beginning of the twelfth century, replaced by the present hideous 'Meccano' bridge, erected temporarily in 1939. To the south by the river at Holme Mill is the prosperous Jordans wholefood mill with visitors' shop. Close by is the beautifully reconstructed

Scroup's Farm. In the mid nineteenth century the river Ivel Navigation ran to Shefford, transporting coal from Pope's Wharf in Biggleswade, but by 1876 the company had been wound up, superseded by the Great Northern Railway. Perhaps Biggleswade's most famous son was Dan Albone (1860-1906), who invented his own bicycles, motorcycles and motor tractors, using the Ivel as his trademark. His workshop is now the Hamilton Cars showroom in Shortmead Street, and there is a riverside picnic place named in his memory almost opposite. From there pleasant walks run beside the Ivel and across the Common to The Lodge, Sandy (Royal Society for the Protection of Birds).

Before leaving the town one should notice a few of the more attractive modern buildings, including the kite-shaped Baptist Church in London Road, the County Library and Stratton School, which is a reminder of the manor house that once existed in Stratton Park.

Church of St Andrew, page 64.

In the locality: The Lodge, page 54; the Shuttleworth Collection, page 95; the Swiss Garden, page 88; and churches at Astwick, page 63; Edworth, page 68; and Old Warden, page 75.

Bletsoe

'I am much in love with Bedfordshire,' wrote Edward Fitzgerald, who, with William Thackeray, spent several summers staying in Bletsoe. Leaving the main road at the Falcon, a pleasant but much restored sixteenth-century coaching inn, one turns to the quieter byways around St Mary's church. The triangle of allotments used to be the village green. Some of the houses date from the fifteenth century, and there are three rows of terraced cottages which were built by the St John family in the eighteenth and nineteenth centuries: two timber-framed and thatched or tiled, the other of brick and slate. Next to the church is the old National (church) School of 1852.

Many of the medieval earthworks of Bletsoe Castle have been destroyed since Wadmore recorded them in 1920. What we see today is only one side of a large courtyard house of the late sixteenth century, now two storeys high, with the whole of the upper range missing. Lady Margaret Beaufort, mother of Henry VII, was born in a house on the site in 1443, and her half-brother John St John inherited Bletsoe in 1482. His descendants lived there until they moved to Melchbourne in 1608.

Church of St Mary, page 64.

Blunham

A bridge with two humps like a camel spans the Ivel, checking one's approach from the A1. A group of thatched cottages beside the church is of considerable age, Shoe Cottage dating from 1666 and The Ovens from 1699. The Ragged Staff was once an inn. The village is small but has two chapels. The Old Meeting Baptist Church in High Street was built of orange brick in 1751. Since then the roof has been raised and a gallery added, supported on cast-iron pillars. In the tree-lined chapel yard are tombstones of the late eighteenth and nineteenth centuries. When the John Donne Lower School was rethatched a few years ago the pupils sealed their names in a bottle which is hidden in the eaves. One building in the village has to be seen to be believed: John Usher's Old Vicarage of 1874, constructed in yellow and orange bricks. There is a rare group of prefabs in Station Road – almost the last in the county.

John Donne (1572-1632), the metaphysical poet and preacher, was rector of Blunham from 1622 until his death, and at the same time Dean of St Paul's. In 1626 he gave the village church a gilt silver chalice which still survives. After a serious illness in 1623 he wrote *Devotions*, which contains the famous lines: 'No man is an island, entire of itself' and 'Never send to know for whom the bell tolls; It tolls for thee'. Were they in his mind as he convalesced beside the Ivel at Blunham?

Church of St James or St Edmund, page 64.

Bolnhurst

Bolnhurst is a long, scattered, straggling parish. To the west, and close to a stream, is the isolated church of St Dunstan: a landmark amidst rather characterless rolling agricultural country. Bolnhurst is a good example of a shrunken medieval village. There are moats at Greensbury Farm, where the Grym family held a manor in 1302, Crowhill Farm, which is a medieval hall-house, and Mavourn, where the Francklin family held sway. Part of a moat also surrounds the Old Rectory. Manor Farm stands within a large damaged earthwork which was possibly an iron age plateau fort. Part of this was adapted to form a moat around manorial buildings belonging to the Abbey of Thorney in the middle ages. The Old Plough Inn is timbered and painted pink. After a disastrous fire in 1989, the restorers left their names and telephone numbers engraved on paving slabs at the door! At the crossroads there are a few timber-framed and thatched houses, as well as modern infill.

Church of St Dunstan, page 65.

Brogborough

Brogborough Hill Picnic Site, page 49; Holcot Wood and Woodland Creation Scheme, page 53.

Bromham

With the opening of the bypass, some peace has returned to this stone-built village, which is virtually a dormitory for Bedford. The thirteenth-century bridge, rebuilt in 1813, has twenty-six arches. A chantry chapel for the safety of travellers in danger from thieves and a holy well were situated close to the watermill. There are still plenty of old stone houses in the village. East, beside the river, is Bromham Hall, a late sixteenth-century brick building, since plaster-rendered, and the home of the ardent Royalist Sir Lewis Dyve. Later it passed to the Trevor family, one of whom, Thomas Trevor, was responsible for the park in which it stands and the church.

Bromham Mill, page 82; **Bromham Mill Picnic Site**, page 49; **church of St Owen**, page 65.

Caddington

Half a dozen roads and tracks meet at Caddington green, an attractive area of grass surrounded by undistinguished buildings and housing estates. The Chequers Inn and the Cricketers both date from the end of the nineteenth century, although the former was licensed before 1822. The trade of the village in the nineteenth and early twentieth centuries was brick and tile making. Curiously, the pits from which the clay was dug have made Caddington famous throughout the world, not for the bricks they produced, but for the stone axes of lower palaeolithic times, made by man during a warm period in the ice ages, somewhere between 125,000 and 70,000 years ago. These axes, many of which are in Luton Museum and the British Museum, were discovered by the Dunstable antiquary Worthington Smith between 1890 and 1910. Smith deduced that they had been made by men working beside a small lake, a fact confirmed by re-examination in 1971-2.

All Saints' church might be as early as the twelfth century though it is mostly of the Victorian restoration of 1875. It does have a genuine Norman doorway with zigzag ornament. The Baptist Chapel dates from 1846.

Campton

There is black and white half-timber work and thatch in this little village. Especially attractive is the manor house built by the Ventris family in 1591. Sir Michael Ventris was shot at by Parliamentarians, and the bullet holes still survive in the walls of one of the panelled rooms. Almost opposite is the eighteenth-century rectory, next to All Saints' church.

Church of All Saints, page 65.

Cardington

An attractive village of brick and colour-washed buildings, Cardington is mostly centred on the well-kept green and church. Many cottages still carry the initials SW or JH, recalling the influence of the Whitbreads and Howards. Red-brick almshouses on the green were built by Samuel Whitbread in 1787, as were the Howard Almshouses in Church Lane, with the plaque 'JH 1762, restored SHW 1928'. John Howard's fine eighteenth-century house still stands in Church Lane. He lived there from 1760 until 1790. There are well-kept gardens and an observatory built by a later owner, S. C. Whitbread, and used in the 1840s. There is a Methodist chapel dated 1925 and the Howard Church at Chapel End. St Mary's church was almost entirely rebuilt between 1897 and 1901, only part of the fifteenth-century chancel surviving. In the wall can be seen an Anglo-Saxon grave cover. In the graveyard across the main road from the church is a monument to those killed in the R101 airship disaster in 1930, designed by Sir Albert Richardson.

Airship Sheds, page 97.

Carlton

A walk amongst the delightful stone-built houses of the narrow High Street shows rural England at its best. The Angel and the Fox are old and worth a visit, and notice the eighteenth-century Stayesmore Manor with its Victorian front. St Mary's church is away from the village along the Turvey Road. Benjamin Rogers was rector here from 1720 to 1771. In his diary he records that in 1733 his five-year-old son fell backwards into the pottage pot just as it was boiling, 'the fleshy part of his backside was miserably scalded and threw him into a fever for a week'. The boy survived to live for fifty-nine years. The Baptist chapel, built in 1760, has a burial ground beside it.

Chalgrave

Church of All Saints, page 65.

Chalton

See under Toddington, page 39

Clapham

The church has a fine Saxon tower. North of the village was the Twin Woods wartime airfield, from which the American bandleader Glenn Miller left to fly to France on 15th December 1944. Neither he nor his plane was ever seen again.

Church of St Thomas of Canterbury, page 66.

Clifton

The peace of this interesting little village has been restored with the building of a bypass. In earlier days transport was provided by the River Ivel Navigation canal, which passed on the north side: its course can still be followed along a footpath from the Stanford road to Shefford. There are pleasant houses of the local yellow Arlesey bricks, a number built in rat-trap bond. In Shefford Road two tiny almshouses, built in 1872 with the proceeds of two nonconformist magazines called *The Gleaner* and *The Sower*, have been converted into a private house. Holly Cottage was formerly a Quaker meeting house and once had a

schoolroom adjoining it. In 1807 the rector paid for the setting up of a straw-plait school, and in 1871 an inspector visiting a similar school in the village found '51 children sitting in a room 10 feet square by 7 feet high; the window was shut, the door opened into a small kitchen, and this into a yard, with a filthy drain close to the door, and a pigsty and privy close by'. After entry 'it was impossible to stay in the plaiting room for a minute without a feeling of nausea'. The village pond is delightful when not surrounded by parked cars, and the pump and well (which also serve as a war memorial) are novel but rather self-conscious. Grange Street has attractive old houses set at angles to the road, and a long view of Clifton Manor.

Church of All Saints, page 66.

Clophill

Clophill is one of the most attractive villages of central Bedfordshire. Adjoining the A6 is the Green with the popular Flying Horse and Green Man public houses and the Olde Cottage with eyebrow windows. On the south side are the village lock-up and pound. In the High Street are seventeenth- and eighteenth-century cottages and Georgian houses some-

The lock-up and village pound at Clophill.

what higher in the social scale. Look out for The Croft, numbers 36 and 45, Mill House and the finest of all, Clophill House, eighteenth-century red brick with tiled roof and panelled parapet with urns. Ivy House is also eighteenth-century, and King's Cottage possibly seventeenth-century. New St Mary's church was built in 1848 in a purely archaeological style. Old St Mary's, on a hilltop 3/4 mile (1.2 km) away, was fourteenth-century, restored in 1819, but is now in ruins. It is preserved by the Bedfordshire County Council, somewhat inappropriately as a picnic site. Enjoy walking up Mill Lane, noticing The Strand and Gothic Blair Cottage. April Cottage is at the top of The Slade with heathland beyond. In Back Street the Stone Jug is a pleasant hostelry. East of the village are seventeenth-century houses at Beadlow, and south-east is the superb motte and bailey castle of Cainhoe.

Cainhoe Castle, page 59; **Deadman's Hill Picnic Site**, page 50.

Cockayne Hatley
Church of St John the Baptist, page 66.

Colmworth
The tall spire of St Denys's church beckons one to this scattered village with its numerous 'ends'. There is the usual mixture of new and old houses, one or two of real merit. One senses a feeling of enclosure in the village, which is the most important element in an otherwise prairie landscape. Near the church is Manor Farm House, on a raised mound with traces of a moat around it. The present house was begun by the Dyers in 1609 and was partly rebuilt at the end of the nineteenth century. Moat House on the other side of the church drive also has a good moat. Such features were not necessarily for defence: they often provided a water supply, aided drainage or acted as fishponds. At the southern end of the village is the splendid medieval building of Low Farm, definitely a place to stand and stare.

Bushmead Priory, page 82; **church of St Denys**, page 67.

Cople
Church of All Saints, page 67.

Cranfield
Cranfield is a long and large village made up of many 'ends', most of which have been absorbed by modern housing. There are three thatched Quaker almshouses close to the Methodist church (rebuilt 1834) and two blocks of Goodman almshouses in High Street. The village pump stands on the green near the Swan Inn, and the holy well with its medicinal properties still flows along the path from Bowling Green Lane to the back of the rectory.

In the 1930s Cranfield aerodrome was built. It played an important part in the Second World War and in 1947 became Cranfield College of Aeronautics, now Cranfield University.

The church, dedicated to St Peter and St Paul, has a very worn Norman doorway in the north wall, and there is an eroded carving, possibly of the Virgin, above the south door. The remainder dates from the thirteenth to fifteenth centuries.

Dean
In both Upper Dean and Lower Dean one's impressions are of lots of modern houses outnumbering older cottages, pleasantly strung out along narrow lanes. There is plenty of timber and thatch, ranging from the minute Old Mill Cottage with its Gothic windows to the large seventeenth-century Dean House Farm and Lodge Farm, both with pitched tiled roofs and sharply pointed gables. Between the buildings are plenty of trees, giving a rural feeling to both villages.

On 17th March 1317 John le Long burgled the house of Maud Bolle in Dean and stole a ham. Maud surprised him and he fell from his ladder. William the Cobbler found his body with a broken neck.

Duloe
See under Staploe, page 35.

Dunstable
Early closing Thursday; market days Wednesday and Saturday.

The prehistoric Icknield Way passes through Dunstable. Above it on the edge of the famous Downs are the Five Knolls, prehistoric

Dunstable Priory church, where Katharine of Aragon was tried.

burial mounds. Bronze and iron age settlements lay on the northern edge of the town. The Roman Watling Street crossed the Icknield Way, and the posting station of *Durocobrivis* was founded there. A cemetery of the third, fourth and perhaps fifth centuries AD suggests that it was a very small and somewhat disorganised settlement, perhaps a wooden shanty town beside the main roads. Another cemetery of the late sixth century belonged to an even smaller Saxon community. Indeed, Dunstable failed to develop as a town until it was deliberately created by Henry I in the early twelfth century. It was never walled but surrounded by a ditch, with the royal lodge of Kingsbury as its nucleus. As a town it lacked water and had to rely on wells dug deep into the chalk. The new town had a school from the beginning, and it is recorded that Geoffrey of Gorham taught there, and 'made a certain play of St Katherine, which we call a miracle play'. 'To give it splendour' he borrowed choir capes from St Albans Abbey. Unfortunately, the night after the play Geoffrey's house burnt down, together with the borrowed capes.

In 1131 the Augustinian priory of St Peter was founded and the town was given to the canons. It is unlikely that anything remains above ground of the monastery, though a room in the Georgian Priory in High Street South might be a survival. A Dominican priory was also founded in 1259 and dissolved in May 1539. Excavations on the site in 1965 uncovered a gold and enamel swan-shaped brooch, now in the British Museum. An Eleanor cross once stood at the corner of West Street and High Street North, recalling the funeral procession of 1290. Henry VIII chose the Augustinian priory as the place of trial for Katharine of Aragon, who was living at Ampthill. Cranmer pronounced the sentence of divorce in the church on 23rd May 1533.

Dunstable was to remain small until the twentieth century, although its position on the Watling Street made it an important coaching stop, with numerous inns. Straw plaiting and hatmaking developed in the town but were overtaken by Luton, where domestic workshops flourished. In the twentieth century printing and engineering have developed and the town has expanded considerably in size.

The church of St Peter is all that remains of Henry I's priory. The Saracen's Head is the oldest surviving public house in the town, some four hundred years old. To the south are the Cart Almshouses of 1723 and Chew's House (1715), originally a school for forty Church of England boys. There is a genuine penny-farthing bicycle outside Charlie Cole's

This School was erected
and ENDOWED by
M⁰FRANCES ASHTON.
M⁰JANE CART and
M⁰THOMAS AYNSCOMBE.
Heirs at Law to Wᴹ CHEW Esq.
ANNO DOM 1715.

Chew's House in Dunstable was once a boys' school.

shop at 105 High Street South. Towards the central crossroads is Middle Row, where market stalls were replaced by shops in the later sixteenth century. On the north side of West Street are refronted timber-framed buildings, some as old as the sixteenth century. In High Street North is the Anchor Arch, an early seventeenth-century gateway which probably led into the Anchor Inn. In the main banking hall of the Nationwide Building Society's office at 20 High Street North are displayed wall paintings of about 1600, discovered when the previous building on the site was demolished in 1985. The Old Sugar Loaf is a coaching inn dating from 1717, and slightly later is Grove House, also once an inn. The Ashton Middle School was the Ashton Grammar School, opened in 1888, and endowed by Francis Ashton in 1728. In Church Street, eighteenth-century Kingsbury Court, the Old Palace Lodge and the Norman King stand on the site of Henry I's lodge. The Ladies' Lodge, originally stone-faced but now painted white, is almshouses endowed by Blandina Marshe in 1743. In the gallery of the public library is a small permanent display illustrating the history of the town.

Amongst various newer buildings are the Queensway Hall (1962-4), the shopping centre with its abstract concrete mural by William Mitchell, and the Church of Our Lady Immaculate (1961-4), which is circular, with a spire. Beyond the southern boundary of the town (in Caddington parish) is the new education campus housing the Manshead Upper School (1971), Streetfield Middle School (1976) and St Mary's Roman Catholic Lower School (1971).

There is a golf course on Dunstable Downs, with the London Gliding Club below, and plenty of room for walking and picnics.

Church of St Peter, page 67; **Dunstable and Whipsnade Downs**, page 50; **Five Knolls**, page 60; **Sewell Cutting**, page 56.

In the locality: Whipsnade Wild Animal Park, page 98; churches at Eaton Bray, page 68; and Kensworth, page 71.

Eaton Bray

Famous in the nineteenth century for its straw plait and its carnations, Eaton Bray stretches for some 2 miles (3 km), a mixture of stone, brick, timber and thatch houses and modern infill, interspersed with orchards. The oldest houses are at Eaton Green on the north, where the street known as The Rye is of particular interest. The old White Horse Inn and the Five Bells stand at the northern crossroads, whilst the Chequers is on the green near Moor End. At Park Farm is one of the finest moated sites in the county with slight traces of William de Cantilupe's castle, built in 1221 and described as 'a serious danger to Dunstable and the neighbourhood'. Seventeenth-century Bellows Mill at the southern end of the village has been carefully preserved.

Church of St Mary, page 68.

Edworth

Although this is a tiny parish, earthworks near the church suggest that a larger village once existed. The Manor is a pleasant seventeenth-century house with timber frame, and the dovecote nearby is of the same date. The Old Rectory is also seventeenth-century, but much restored. One house, drastically modernised, but of more than passing interest, is Beaumonts', along the Manor drive from the Hinxworth road. It was the home of young Agnes Beaumont, a girl with an infatuation for John Bunyan. In February 1674 Bunyan was preaching at Gamlingay, and Agnes persuaded him, against his will, to let her ride on the back of his horse to the meeting. Her father objected violently, to no avail. When Agnes returned home she found herself locked out of the house and had to spend a freezing night in a barn. A few days later Mr Beaumont died suddenly, and Agnes was accused of murdering him by witchcraft. She was tried but fortunately acquitted and lived to a good age.

Church of St George, page 68.

Eggington

Eggington is a delightful little village composed of well-built yellow and orange brick cottages, with here and there evidence of timber frames and nogging, and roofs of thatch or pleasant orange tile. The Horseshoes Inn is near the centre of the village, with a Wesleyan chapel opposite. Parts of the house called Claridges must be at least sixteenth-century in date. Eggington House is a splendid building of 1696, three storeys high and divided into seven bays, with urns above on a parapet. St Michael's church is fourteenth-century and

heavily restored internally. The font might be thirteenth-century. The bell turret is Victorian.

On the crest of the hill above the brook at **Clipston** is a small cruck house with brick infill, and unfortunately a green corrugated iron roof. Cruck buildings are amongst the earliest in Britain. It is best seen in winter when the chestnut is not in leaf.

Elstow

This was John Bunyan's village, and parts of it look much as they did in his day. On the large green is the Moot Hall. Beside it is the church where Bunyan rang the bells, and close by is the High Street, where he lived (though his house has now gone). The site of his birthplace is near Harrowden (OS 153: TL 063472), in Elstow parish, and is marked by a stone. Much of the village was owned by the Whitbread family, who gave the Moot Hall to the village in 1950 and in 1974 sold the fine timber-framed row of cottages to the Borough Council for £1. These have now been splendidly restored and consist of hall and cross-wing houses, a Wealden hall and a merchant's house. Little remains of the Benedictine nunnery founded at Elstow in 1078. In 1616 much of its stone was used to build a manor house for Thomas Hillersdon, the ruins of which are beside the church. On the western border of the parish lay Bedford Racecourse, popular between 1730 and 1874.

Church of St Mary, page 68; **Elstow Moot Hall**, page 93.

Eversholt

Eversholt is a village with ten 'ends' and no obvious centre. There are many attractive old houses, like Witts End Close, which was almost derelict but has been restored. Around the church are grouped the Green Man (1835), the Old Bakery, the magnificent early eighteenth-century Church Farm and the School House with its fine porch, where Frank Wild, one of Shackleton's Arctic companions, grew up. The nearby cricket ground is the envy of many villages.

Church of St John, page 68.

Everton

Church of St Mary, page 69.

Restored medieval houses in Elstow.

Eyeworth

This is a small roadside village of yellow brick Victorian houses, with wide views looking eastwards over large fields towards Cambridgeshire and the infant river Cam forming its boundary. The chimneys and gables of Church Farm suggest that its is of seventeenth-century date. All Saints' church, partly built in the fourteenth century, mainly of brown cobble, was struck by lightning in 1967 and its fifteenth-century spire was destroyed. A few days later thieves stole the lead from the roof. Inside are a number of brasses and monuments to the Anderson family, some of which were mutilated during the Commonwealth. Sir Edmund Anderson (died 1605) was a judge at the trial of Mary, Queen of Scots. Outside on the church sills are medieval graffiti, fast disappearing on the weathered Totternhoe stone.

Farndish

Tucked into the extreme north-west of the county is this delightfully remote little hamlet of less than a dozen houses, all in good limestone and, until recently, Collyweston slate roofing. Grange Farm, with mullioned windows, is late seventeenth-century, and the Alderman's House was built in 1689. St Michael's church is basically thirteenth-century. Now in the care of the Redundant Churches Fund, it is famous for its lovely south doorway of 1210, with its chequered bands of chocolate-coloured ironstone and buff limestone. Corbel faces gaze down from the south wall, in one of the most secluded corners of Bedfordshire.

Felmersham

Felmersham is a visual delight. St Mary's church, on a spur above the river bridge, seems a natural focus, although to the casual visitor the village seems to lack a centre. The fourteenth-century tithe barn has been cleverly adapted for housing. The Crown, the Six Ringers and the rebuilt Plough are all popular hostelries. Historically the village is best-known for its Celtic bronzes found in a local gravel pit and now in Bedford Museum.

Church of St Mary, page 69; **Felmersham Gravel Pits**, page 51.

Flitton

The de Grey Mausoleum, page 83.

Flitwick

Situated on the main railway line from London to Sheffield, Flitwick has expanded enormously in recent years. The older part of the village lies around the church of St Peter. The Mount is a small castle earthwork on the housing estate to the north of the church (OS 153: TL 027343). There are a few timber-framed and brick cottages in Church Road. Flitwick Manor, which was built in the seventeenth and eighteenth centuries, was once the home of the Brooks family. It is now an exclusive hotel and restaurant with its own helicopter pad.

Church of St Peter, page 69; **Flitwick Moor**, page 51; **Flitwick Wood**, page 51.

Goldington

See under Bedford, page 9.

Gravenhurst

The parishes of Upper and Lower Gravenhurst were united in 1888. The hilltop village of Upper Gravenhurst has a few old houses around the church. St Giles's was heavily restored in Victorian times but has Norman work in the nave walls and blocked north door. Seventeenth-century Cart's Farm was the property of the Jane Cart charity of Dunstable from 1736 until 1920. Lower Gravenhurst is on a lower hill to the southwest.

Church of Our Lady, Lower Gravenhurst, page 73.

Great Barford

Great Barford is more closely related to the river than the majority of Ouse-side villages in the county, because the houses come down to the river and paths beside the water draw the visitor. The river is navigable here and the lock was reopened in 1976. The bridge of seventeen arches was built in the fifteenth century, though the parapet is more recent. At its end is the Anchor Inn, Bridge House of sixteenth-century date, Bridge Cottage and River Cottage. More pleasing buildings stretch up the High Street, especially number 59, a Georgian house with handsome classical pediment.

Greenfield

See under Pulloxhill, page 30.

Harlington

Harlington House is a seventeenth-century timber-framed building with later additions.

The bridge at Felmersham.

The river Great Ouse at Great Barford.

In November 1660 John Bunyan was brought here before Francis Wingate, a justice of the peace, for preaching at Lower Samshill in the adjoining parish. There are a number of attractive timber-framed houses with tile or thatched roofs around the church and in Sundon Road adjoining the Carpenters' Arms. There is an early nineteenth-century mounting stone outside the latter. North-east of the village at Upper East End is the oak tree, now dead, from which Bunyan is alleged to have preached. A sapling has been planted beside it (OS 166: TL 046313).

Church of St Mary, page 69.

Harrold

The village is large and alive, with plenty of limestone and thatch, and warm orange brick here and there. The Old Manor of about 1600 stands in the High Street. On the triangular tree-filled green is the octagonal eighteenth-century market house or butter cross, and behind it is a neat circular stone lock-up of

1824. The Magpie and the Oakley Arms vie for trade. Running north from the latter is Brook Lane with a little stream and too many parked cars. The leather-dressing industry flourished in the village for a hundred years but came to an end in 1983.

Church of St Peter, page 69; Forty Foot Lane Picnic Site, page 52; Harrold-Odell Country Park, page 52.

Heath and Reach

Stop by the Green at Heath and Reach and see the village at its best. Close your eyes to the tasteless Wesleyan chapel of 1877 and the hideous web of overhead cables, and enjoy the Victorian red brick pumphouse of 1873, the Duke's Head with thatch, and the unpretentious seventeenth- and eighteenth-century cottage ranges to the west. A walk along Lanes End will reveal some exciting cottages with splendid gardens.

Unfortunately, St Leonard's church of 1829 is truly ugly. The sixteenth-century stone tower cannot save it, and the rest is Victorian brick at its most indifferent. The views from the water tower are fine, but the extensive sand workings quite demoralising. You may regain your composure in Stockgrove Country Park.

Stockgrove Country Park, page 58.

Henlow

A beautifully neat village, Henlow consists mainly of good brick houses built in the last three centuries, whose varied roof lines make a walk along the High Street and Park Lane delightful. St Mary's church, set back beyond a reclaimed quarry, is more interesting externally than within. There is a pleasant walk from the church, in front of Henlow Grange, to the busy A507. One passes the eighteenth-century gatehouses of the Grange and the attractive Henlow Middle School, to see the fine mansion, built in brick about 1700, and guarded by tall iron railings and gates. There is an air of dereliction about the surrounding park, in stark contrast to the carefully maintained lawns of the school and Boyd Memorial Playing Field. The modern Methodist church is worth a second glance.

Once the old Midland Railway line from Hitchin to Bedford ran through the south of the parish with a station slightly east of the RAF Henlow Camp roundabout. This was one reason for establishing a repair depot for Eastern Command in 1918, which began Henlow's long association with the RAF. Part of St Mary's churchyard is used for the burial of RAF personnel.

Higham Gobion

Church of St Margaret, page 69.

Hinwick

There is a delightful approach along the avenue of limes known as The Slade. A narrow lane leads up into the village, where old stone cottages cluster around the tiniest possible 'square'. To the north stands the four-square yellow block of Hinwick House. It is occasionally open to the public during the summer: telephone 01933 53624 for details. It is a most pleasing classical building erected between 1709 and 1714 for Richard Orlebar, who might have been his own architect. Almost every detail of its construction is recorded, including the cost of building it: £3848 4s 9d. High on the south front is a pediment by John Hart depicting the goddess Diana.

Westward down the lane is Hinwick Hall with its Country Crafts and Garden Centre.

The village lock-up at Harrold.

However, it was better known as one of the Shaftesbury Society's earliest residential schools for physically handicapped children and is now a College of Further Education for disabled teenagers. The hall dates from about 1540 on the west side, but a new eastern front was built early in the eighteenth century using the local limestone and probably the same craftsmen as Hinwick House.

Honeydon

See under Staploe, page 35.

Houghton Conquest

Church of All Saints, page 70; Kingswood and Glebe Meadows, page 54.

Houghton Regis

Sewell Cutting, page 56.

Hulcote

Church of St Nicholas, page 70.

Ickwell

First impressions are of an extensive green, dominated by a large oak tree. Closer investi-

gation reveals a number of colour-washed thatched or tiled cottages, some over-restored, as well as pleasant brick houses of the seventeenth and eighteenth centuries. 'Upon this spot, in a blacksmith's shop, was Tompion brought up; who from making plough-chains, took in clocks to repair: and so followed the watchmaking line, till he attained the highest excellence.' So wrote Byng, the diarist, in 1790 of Ickwell's most famous son, Thomas Tompion (1639-1703), described as 'the father of English watchmakers' (see page 105). The smithy is still beside the green, his cottage is the first in Upper Caldecote Road, and his grave is in Westminster Abbey. There is a permanent maypole on the green; in former days celebrations around it lasted two months. Today village cricket is the more normal sight during the summer.

May Day celebrations, page 106.

Kempston

Palaeolithic flint implements were found here in the nineteenth century. Aerial photographs have revealed a cursus or ceremonial way of about 2500 BC in the Hill Grounds area. A Roman villa and Saxon cemetery were ex-

Hinwick House, home of the Orlebar family from 1709.

cavated near All Saints' church in 1992. Another large Saxon cemetery has given its name to the Saxon Shopping Centre. The barracks, completed in 1876, drew new development, which led to infilling from Bedford to Kempston and the swallowing of old buildings amongst the mediocrity of the new. West of the main village numerous 'ends' have survived relatively unspoilt and worthy of inspection. In Kempston High Street the King William IV inn is most likely to catch the eye with its spectacular black and white walls and tiled roof. It is medieval in origin, but most of what we see today dates from the mid seventeenth century. Almost opposite, The Barns is of the same date, though rough-cast and colour-washed. Pedestrians may walk along Water Lane, with its ford and small stream, and then follow The Causeway beside the Ouse to Church End, where All Saints' church stands. The Church of the Transfiguration was consecrated in 1940. It was designed by J. Harrold Gibbons in 1929 and is a late example of the Arts and Crafts movement.

Church of St Mary, page 71.

Kensworth

The main settlement is at Kensworth Common, strung out along the B4540 and exhibiting few buildings of distinction. Church End is half a mile (800 metres) to the north up a very steep hill, with an attractive group of trees and farm buildings around St Mary's church. A winding lane leads east to Kensworth Lynch, where half-timbered houses of the seventeenth and eighteenth centuries surround Lynch House, a pleasing brick building of the late eighteenth century. Chequers Cottage was originally a public house, and on the Watling Street stands the Pack Horse inn, which dates at least from the eighteenth century and was once called the Orange Tree. The Kensworth farms used large donkey wheels to draw water from the wells of the area, which were often 60 metres (200 feet) deep. A wheel from Nash Farm, 4.5 metres (15 feet) in diameter, can be seen outside Luton Museum, in Wardown Park.

Church of St Mary, page 71.

Keysoe

Church of St Mary, page 71.

Knotting

Church of St Margaret, page 72.

Leagrave

Waulud's Bank, page 62.

Leighton Buzzard

Early closing Thursday; market days Tuesday and Saturday.

Prehistoric and Roman remains have come from the parish, and three Saxon cemeteries were found at Chamberlain's Barn sand quarries. The name 'Leighton' comes from the old English 'garden where leeks are grown'. 'Buzzard' is a corruption of the name of Theobald de Busar or Busat, Leighton's first prebendary (1189-99). Leighton is mentioned as a royal manor in Domesday Book. There is reason to think this manor lay on the southern edge of the parish south of Grovebury Farm by 1155. Building foundations identified as both a Benedictine priory and a royal manor have been excavated in the area but are now destroyed. The joy and glory of Leighton is All Saints' church with its tall spire.

After the church, the Market Cross is the oldest structure in the town. Dating from the early fifteenth century, it is 8.2 metres (27 feet) high and was restored in 1852-3. Opposite the cross stands the Swan Hotel, built around 1840. There are numerous old buildings in the High Street, and these continue into the early Victorian Church Square. In North Street is the Friends' Meeting House of 1789, and beyond are the yellow brick Wilkes Almshouses founded by Edward Wilkes in 1633 and rebuilt in 1857. Leighton is a town in which one should cast one's eyes upward towards the roof lines, where medieval timber framing can often be detected. Not all is ancient. The town is blessed with an excellent library, theatre and lecture rooms. There are pleasant parks in the town, especially Parson's Close, and further south Paynes Park, where the Leighton Buzzard Railway is situated.

Beating the Bounds, page 106; **church of All Saints**, page 73; **Leighton Buzzard Rail-**

way, page 97; **Leighton Lady Cruises**, page 97.

In the locality: Stockgrove Country Park, page 58; church at Tilsworth, page 79.

Linslade

Linslade dates from Victorian times and is undistinguished, although there are some attractive mid-Victorian town houses near the parish church of St Barnabas, the latter designed by Benjamin Ferrey in 1848 and containing two windows by Kempe. The ancient church of St Mary lies well to the north of the modern town. It stands in a well-kept churchyard with excellent gravestones. The west tower dates from the fifteenth century. Inside is a late Norman font with scroll and animal decoration. Close to the chancel arch is a very unusual early thirteenth-century seat, with stone arms and a semicircular arch above. There is also an interesting brass to a gentleman who enjoyed three wives. Beyond the churchyard wall, and close to the

The Market Cross in Leighton Buzzard, from an engraving of 1853.

canal, is the handsome early eighteenth-century Manor Farmhouse in red and vitreous brick.

In the locality: see under Leighton Buzzard, page 25.

Lower Gravenhurst

See under Gravenhurst, page 21.
Church of Our Lady, page 73.

Lower Stondon

Stondon Transport Museum and Garden Centre, page 96.

Luton

Early closing Wednesday; market (covered) Monday to Saturday.

Luton is the largest town in the county, with a population of over 174,000. In spite of its brash modern appearance and seemingly endless housing estates, Luton has a considerable history. Beside the Icknield Way to the north were successive prehistoric settlements (see Waulud's Bank, page 62). There was a small Romano-British village, which was destroyed by fire, in the area of Runfold Avenue, and early Saxon cemeteries in Argyll Avenue. The Britons and West Saxons fought a battle at Limbury in AD 571, and the area was divided by the Danelaw boundary of AD 886. In the tenth century it was claimed as a royal township, and Edward the Elder began building a church, completed by Aethelstan about 930. Castles were built by Robert de Waudari in 1139 and Falkes de Breauté in 1216, but neither building has survived. The oldest known house is the Moat House at Limbury, built between 1370 and 1400. St Mary's church represents the medieval glory of Luton. In the seventeenth century nonconformity became popular in the town, as it did throughout Bedfordshire, and in 1698 Thomas Marsom built the first Baptist meeting in Luton in Park Street; its successor was replaced by a new building in 1986.

The straw-hat industry had begun in Luton by the mid seventeenth century and many Bedfordshire villages were involved in plaiting straw. During the next century and a half the trade flourished, with Luton at its centre. With the late arrival of the railway in 1858 hat manufacture rapidly expanded. A decline began with the First World War, when most of the export trade was lost, and this continued in 1931 when supplies of Asian straw ceased. Felt-hat manufacture, begun about 1870, increased and by 1939 the firm of Stuart Hubbard was the largest in the world. Today the firm has gone and the industry is much reduced in size, but the wearing of hats by younger ladies of the royal family is creating a new interest.

As a twentieth-century engineering town Luton was world-famous, especially for Vauxhall cars and trucks, Electrolux, SKF (UK) Limited and George Kent's. Today only Vauxhall is still actively engaged in assembling cars. Luton Airport, opened in 1938, is famous as an international airport specialising in the package holiday trade.

Regrettably Luton today is an untidy large industrial town, bursting at its seams, with almost every scrap of land sacrificed to the glory of mammon. Yet for those who wish to linger there are things to see. Avoid the claustrophobic plastic shopping centre and turn immediately to the quiet sanctity of St Mary's church. It is hemmed in by the uninspired buildings of the University.

In George Street is the Red Lion Hotel, Luton's oldest inn, which originated around 1540. At the opposite end is the Town Hall, a typical monument to defiant civic pride, built between 1934 and 1938 to replace one angrily burnt down by townsfolk in 1919. The figure of Courage on the war memorial holding aloft the palm of Victory is by Sir Hamo Thornycroft (1922). In George Street West are the last remaining fine town houses of the nineteenth-century plait masters. By the Chapel Street roundabout is the former Union Chapel of 1836-44, one of the more elegant buildings of the town, now divided into flats. Proceed along Castle Street to Hibbert Street to see the Queen Anne style almshouses, built in 1885 for twelve women by the philanthropist Robert Hibbert, whose wealth came from the sugar plantations of Jamaica. Return to the town centre to visit the Public Library in St George's Square. When it was opened in 1962 it incorporated the latest concepts in library design, but now

it is looking a little tired and its shelves decidely empty. It has a small theatre on the third floor.

A car is needed now to drive to Wardown Park along the tree-lined New Bedford Road. The entrance to the car park for the fine Luton Museum is in Old Bedford Road. Further along the road is the Sixth Form College designed by Marshall and Tweedy in 1936 in the modern International style with open planning instead of cloisters. A vast accretion of new buildings has destroyed much of the harmony of the original design. 'Bide-a-While' garden in New Bedford Road is a delight for those with horticultural interests. A unique house in Luton is 22 Lansdowne Road, designed by Edgar L. Barber in the Arts and Crafts style in the 1920s. The late fourteenth-century thatched Moat House (now a restaurant) is not far away in Nunnery Lane, whilst Luton's only other thatched cottage (seventeenth-century and excessively restored) is in Butterfield Green Road at Stopsley.

Finally two modern churches are worth a visit. St Andrew's in Blenheim Crescent has a massive buttressed light brick tower, vaguely reminiscent of Scandinavian architecture between the world wars, and is by Sir Giles Gilbert Scott (1931-2). Its narrow windows and concrete arches give it an air of calm dignity. At Round Green is St Christopher's by Bedfordshire's adopted architect Sir Albert Richardson. This intimate and friendly brick and timber church of 1936-7 is one of only two that he designed in their entirety, although he restored many. In Stopsley the new Baptist church (1994), with its vast pyramidal roof, dominates St Thomas's Road.

Bradger's Hill, page 49; **Bramingham Wood**, page 49; **church of St Mary**, page 73; **Dallow Downs**, page 50; **Galley and Warden Hills**, page 52; **John Dony Field Centre**, page 94; **London Luton International Airport**, page 98; **Luton Hoo**, page 86; **Luton Museum and Art Gallery**, page 94; **Stockwood Craft Museum and Gardens and Mossman Collection**, page 95; **Waulud's Bank**, page 62.

In the locality: Someries Castle, page 87; Woodside Farm and Wildlife Park, page 100.

Marston Moretaine

Marston Thrift, page 55; Stewartby Lake Country Park, page 57.

Maulden

Maulden Wood, page 55.

Melchbourne

Early in the thirteenth century the Knights Hospitallers attempted to create a tiny town at Melchbourne, which had the right to hold a weekly Friday market, and a fair on the vigil, feast and morrow of St Mary Magdalene (21st to 23rd July). The town failed and much of it was deserted. Many earthworks north-east of the church reveal the site of the preceptory of the Knights and the abandoned house platforms of the settlement.

Today it is a strange village with no real centre, in a well-wooded area, and dominated by St Mary's church and Melchbourne House. The latter, a somewhat gaunt mansion, was built about 1610 for Lord St John, and remodelled in 1741. It has extensive parks with two ornamental lakes. A feature of the village is The Street, a terrace of thatched cottages, some with blue doors, dating from the early eighteenth century. A second row was destroyed by a pyromaniac in the 1960s. The church was rebuilt in Georgian style in 1779, but the tower is basically medieval. The Jacobean north porch is believed to have come from Woodford in Northamptonshire. It is furnished with box pews, including the St John family pew in the chancel, with its own fireplace. The lavish Oakley Hunt kennels were built in 1973 at Cock Lane (TL 015642), south-west of the village.

Melchbourne Bird Gardens, page 98.

Meppershall

A plateau village, much suburbanised, Meppershall has a long dull street leading west to St Mary's church and the Manor House. Close by is one genuine half-timbered cottage on an attractive, but dangerous, bend in the road. The Manor House is one of the finer timber-framed buildings in the county, with characteristics of west country half-timber detailing. It has two big gables and three smaller ones between. Decorating the front are a thistle and crown in raised plasterwork. The building is partially surrounded by a moat. Beyond it are the castle earthworks known as The Hills. From this end of the village one gets the most magnificent view of the Bedfordshire range of the Chiltern escarpment. Little wonder that a villa appears to have been built here in Roman times. St Mary's church consists of an early twelfth-century tower base and transepts, with a restored thirteenth-century chancel. The nave and aisles are Victorian, by Bloomfield. There are remnants of brasses to John Meppershall (died 1440) and John Boteler (died 1441), and a somewhat primitive monument to a former rector, Timothy Archer (died 1672).

East of the village at Chapel Farm are the remains of St Thomas's Chapel, built soon after 1175 by Gilbertine monks from Chicksands Priory. The nave is of Norman date, the chancel sixteenth-century. Particularly fine is the late Norman north doorway with bold geometric carving. Used as a barn and not open to the general public, it can usually be visited on application to the farm.

The Hills, page 61.

Millbrook

Millbrook is a pleasant little village set beside a steep hill with enormous views, and crowned by St Michael's church. Bunyan's Valley of Humiliation to the west is dominated by General Motors' vast testing ground.

Church of St Michael, page 74.

Milton Bryan

This little village is in two parts: Church End clusters around the church and consists mainly of modern houses, with a few older ones ; South End lies along the Toddington road and contains a number of excellently restored timber-framed houses, the popular Red Lion pub and the former post office cottage, partly supported on three wooden beams. The area around the Town Pond in the cul-de-sac to the south is worth exploring.

Church of St Peter, page 74.

Northill

This is one of the most attactive villages south of the Ouse. A pleasing group beside the

South End at Milton Bryan.

village pond includes the church, the Crown Inn, a row of eighteenth-century thatched cottages and The Grange of about 1700, with a shell-shaped door hood on carved brackets. Behind the church is the red-brick rectory. **Church of St Mary**, page 75.

Oakley

Apart from the church, Oakley is an architectural disappointment. Most of the village belonged to the Dukes of Bedford, who considered the local limestone buildings unhygienic and swept most of them away in favour of red brick houses roofed in tile and slate. Substantially built, each is decorated with a coronet and letter B. Of old buildings, the Bedford Arms is much restored. Beside it stand Queen's College Farm, Middle Farm and two other houses, which form an interesting group. By the church are Rectory Cottage and St Mary's Cottage, and below them, over the Great Ouse, is a narrow bridge built for the eighth Duke of Bedford in 1813. Oakley House, remodelled by Henry Holland for the fifth Duke as a hunting lodge, is not open to the public.

In 1707 the parishioners gathered in the field below the church to watch the swimming of a witch. Twice the woman was ducked in the river, and twice her clothes prevented her from sinking, causing the onlookers to assume her guilty. However, when she was weighed against the church Bible the verdict turned in her favour and she was released, although very few present believed her innocent. **Church of St Mary**, page 75.

Odell

Odell is a small attractive Ouse-side village of limestone and brick, strung out along the High Street. Beside the tiny green the upper floor of the Bell bulges frighteningly outwards. Village Farm at the west end is a tall house of three floors with a good orange pantiled barn beyond. Opposite is Linden House of whitewashed stone with the date 1777 on the chimney. Some of the modern infilling seems insensitive and unnecessary in this tiny village. Odell Castle began as a Norman motte built by Walter de Wahull. The present house was built in 1962 on the old castle mound.

Peter Bulkley, the rector from 1620 to 1635, was suspected of Puritanism and deprived of the living. He followed the Pilgrim Fathers to Massachusetts, where he founded the town of Concord.

Church of All Saints, page 75; **Harrold-Odell Country Park**, page 52.

Old Warden

Described in 1899 as looking like a stage set, the village was mainly the creation in the nineteenth century of the third Lord Ongley, who attempted to create a village in the fashionable picturesque style with certain Swiss features. We are told that he insisted on the village women dressing in tall hats and red cloaks. There are numerous delightful and unspoiled thatched cottages, rusticated well-houses and all the trimmings required of a *village ornée* set at angles and heights amongst the trees. North of the village stands St Leonard's church.

Church of St Leonard, page 75; **Old Warden Tunnel**, page 55; **the Shuttleworth Collection**, page 95; **the Swiss Garden**, page 88.

Pavenham

Pavenham is one of the most exciting of the Ouse valley villages, set on a well-wooded river terrace at the base of which locally used rushes and osiers once grew. Old houses of limestone with thatch or well-worn tiles line the High Street. Older cottages stand end-on to the street, River Row and Monks Row being typical. The new Plaiters Close, built for old people, is well suited to the village. Weavers Lane reminds us of the makers of rush matting, famous here since the mid seventeenth century. Now only decorative baskets are made in Mill Lane.

Church of St Peter, page 75; **Hay Ceremony**, page 106.

Pegsdon

See under Shillington, page 32.
Pegsdon Hills, page 55.

Pertenhall

A quiet village beside the B660, Pertenhall is easily overlooked by the car-borne traveller. The manor house, church and rectory make a splendid group. The white-walled Jacobean manor contains Elizabethan panelling. It is reported that two dozen skeletons were found when the house was restored in the nineteenth century. The Old Rectory has a superb re-strained Georgian front of rubbed red brick of 1799.

Church of St Peter, page 75.

Podington

There are extensive remains of a castle earth-work at Manor Farm; its origin is unknown. This is a tiny village, but its two main streets are a delight with houses of limestone and thatch, some dating from 1680. Estate houses of a century later have arch designs set into their façades. From the church one glimpses a splendid thatched barn to the west. The former Second World War airfield is now the Santa Pod drag-racing circuit, whose hideous drone shatters the peace of the area at weekends.

Church of St Mary, page 76.

Potsgrove

Church of St Mary, page 76.

Potton

Early closing Thursday.

Potton is an attractive little market town of red and yellow brick houses, with numerous older timber-framed and stone buildings. The use of herringbone sandstone walling is a unique local feature. The great fire of Potton destroyed much of the town in 1783. The medieval market square is now enclosed by Georgian buildings, with others of the sixteenth to nineteenth centuries amongst them. The Clock Tower, rebuilt in 1956, replaces the original Shambles. The Rose and Crown (1785) and Sun House (a medieval Wealden house) are only two of many listed historic buildings of note. Walks along Bull Street or Horslow Street are particularly rewarding. Once important for its tanning industry, and more recently market gardening, Potton is now a commuter town with new housing estates. At Deepdale the Locomotive Inn has an interesting collection of railway memorabilia.

Church of St Mary, page 76; **Potton Woods**, page 56.

In the locality: churches at Cockayne Hatley, page 66; and Sutton, page 79.

Pulloxhill

This village crowns the north-eastern end of a ridge from which there are extensive views north and south. Soon after his ordination in 1203 Bishop William de Blois of Lincoln ordained a vicarage in the village, and St James's church was dedicated in 1219. Unfortunately it fell into ruins, but was rebuilt in 1846 by J. T. Wing. Only the eastern end of the chancel survives intact from the thirteenth century. There is a monument to Sir William Briers (died 1653) and his two wives.

The village is pleasant but not exciting, though the late seventeenth-century house opposite the church is worth enjoying. There are too many juxtapositions of attractive and downright ugly buildings for real satisfaction. Upbury Moat to the north-west is one of the best-preserved manorial earthworks in the county and may be part of the manor held by Dunstable Priory. Kitchen End Farm, on the Barton road, should not be missed.

In 1680 a 'gold mine' was discovered at *Pollux Hill* and was seized by Charles II's Society of Mines Royal. It was leased to a refiner, who found 'a heavy yellowish metal like talc. This was reported to contain the gold.' However, it turned out to be 'fools' gold', flakes of mica in glacial drift, and the mine was abandoned. Gold Close still exists today.

Part of **Greenfield** to the north has some good vernacular architecture, especially in Mill Lane. The village was one of the first to be lit by electricity, which was generated by a dynamo worked by a steam engine at the mill. **Centenary Wood**, page 49.

Renhold

Howbury, page 61.

Ridgmont

Segenhoe Old Church, page 86.

Riseley

This is a brick-built village, which is not surprising since bricks were made from at least 1558 and by the mid nineteenth century provided one of the main occupations. There are old and new brick and timber-framed houses, with thatched or tiled roofs, often standing at right angles to the roads. Particularly interesting are numbers 78 and 135 High Street and the Fox and Hounds. The Baptist chapel has been pulled down, but two grave-

stones still stand beside the Keysoe Road. **Church of All Saints**, page 76; **Good Friday Cakes**, page 107.

Roxton

The village sits amongst the flat fields above the Ouse, between the A1 and the A428. There are a number of thatched cottages connected with the Metcalfe estate. Its surprise is the thatched Congregational chapel backing on to Roxton House. Created from a barn in 1808 and improved in 1824, it is unique in the county. The fourteenth-century church of St Mary has a fifteenth-century tower. There are a painted wooden screen with saints and monuments to a fourteenth-century lady and to Roger Hunt, a Speaker of the House of Commons who died in 1438. To the north at Wyboston in 1934 the Land Settlement Association built identical houses on large plots of land in an attempt to attract families from depressed areas of northern England. South of Roxton beside the Ouse stood five bronze age barrows, ploughed in medieval times and destroyed by quarrying after excavation in 1972-4.

Sandy

Early closing Thursday.

A dull town, Sandy is desperately trying to find its own identity. The triangular 'centre' surrounded by old and new shops is scarcely inspiring, but there are old buildings, including thatch and plaster, timber framing and the local sandstone. The best view is from the Pinnacle hill to the east. Sandy rose to fame as a market-gardening town in the sixteenth century, but long before that it had been important in iron age and Roman times. Recent excavations in the present-day cemetery have shown that Sandy was a small Roman town with timber-framed houses, spread along a narrow street. In the centre of the modern town is Sandye Place, built for the Monoux family in the mid eighteenth century and now a Middle School. Its ironstone dovecote can be seen from the churchyard. Towards Everton is Hasells Hall, the eighteenth-century home of the Pyms, with gardens designed by Humphry Repton. The Lodge is the headquarters of the Royal Society for the

Protection of Birds. The Great North Road originally ran through the town, with numerous coaching inns providing food and lodging. The King's Arms still stands as a reminder. **Church of St Swithun**, page 77; **The Lodge**, page 54.

In the locality: Willington Dovecote and Stables, page 88; and churches at Blunham, page 64; Everton, page 69; Northill, page 75; and Tempsford, page 79.

Sewell

The delightfully secluded hamlet of Sewell has regained its tranquillity now that the railway and chalk quarry are closed. It warranted its own entry in Domesday Book and was an early stronghold of the Quakers. Today there are still splendid timber, brick and plaster buildings along the single street. Sewell Cutting is now a nature reserve.

Maiden Bower, page 61; **Sewell Cutting**, page 56.

Sharnbrook

This is a smart, expanding village, with a variety of seventeenth- and eighteenth-century limestone and thatch cottages, interspersed with houses of red brick. Stone-built Tofte Manor, inscribed 1613, is visible from Colworth Road. Set in a 1000 acre (400 hectare) estate is Colworth House, built in the eighteenth century, and now dominated by the new buildings of the vast Unilever Food Research Establishment. Sharnbrook House, built early in the eighteenth century, is now a residential home for the elderly. Stoke Watermill has been converted into a theatre, and the windmill into a private observation tower. Sharnbrook (Solbrook) was the home of H. E. Bates's immortal character Uncle Silas (Joseph Betts), who lived in a thatched cottage at the top of Barleycroft Lane.

Church of St Peter, page 77.

Sharpenhoe

Sharpenhoe Clappers, pages 57 and 62.

Shefford

Early closing Wednesday.

Ancient wealth is reflected in the splendid bronze age beaker found at Shefford, and the contents of two princely late iron age burial vaults accidentally discovered at Stanfordbury Farm. A Roman cemetery lay close to the Robert Bloomfield School site. There is little evidence of Shefford's former importance as a market town which once rivalled Bedford, though two good medieval houses survive, namely Tudor House, in High Street, and Porch House, with its jutting upper floor, in North Bridge Street. In 1822 the Ivel Navigation canalised the river from Biggleswade to Shefford with a series of five locks and a wharf at Shefford, where coal was the main commodity unloaded. The scheme was not a success and by 1876 was wound up. The Midland Railway passed through Shefford when it opened in 1857, but it was closed by Beeching in 1962. Robert Bloomfield, the shoemaker poet, lived in North Bridge Street and died in Shefford on 19th August 1823. He is buried at Campton. St Michael's church was almost entirely rebuilt in 1822 and is unremarkable. The first post-Reformation Roman Catholic chapel to be built in the county was St George's (1791). It was replaced in 1884 by St Francis's, which retained part of the old building as the sacristy. The church is noteworthy for its reredos 9 metres (30 feet) high.

Chicksands Priory, page 82; **Chicksands Wood**, page 50; **Rowney Warren**, page 56; **Shefford Fair**, page 108.

In the locality: the Shuttleworth Collection, page 95; the Swiss Garden, page 88; Stondon Transport Museum and Garden Centre, page 96; and churches at Campton, page 65; Clifton, page 66; Lower Gravenhurst, page 72; and Southill, page 78.

Shelton

This is one of the loveliest little villages in Bedfordshire, with cottages ranged around the church and crossroads. Shelton Hall is now a farmhouse beside the church, with a most pleasing Georgian rectory opposite. One of the tiniest schools in the county is now used as an artist's studio.

Church of St Mary, page 77.

Shillington

Shillington is a large village of local yellow

The Fox inn at Carlton.

Church Farm stands opposite the church at Eversholt.

Medieval Porch House in North Bridge Street, Shefford.

brick, with here and there good timber-framed buildings. The Old Court House at Apsley End, the former Five Bells in Church Street and numerous buildings in Upton End Road are only a few of the delights for those who have time to search. Look down Church Street at what are basically seventeenth-century houses set at all angles and jostling to please the eye. All Saints' church crowns the hill, a landmark for miles.

Pegsdon to the south is undistinguished, except for Bury End Farm and much restored Pegsdon Barns. The chalk hills beyond are some of the finest downs in Bedfordshire, with strip lynchets and a neolithic barrow, Knocking Knoll, to the east.

Church of All Saints, page 77; Church Spanel, page 59; Pegsdon Hills, page 55.

Silsoe

This is a delightful village with white timber-framed cottages in the High Street, each with steps up to the front door. Along Church Road is the lock-up built in 1796 of ironstone, with a stout door and narrow slit window. St James's church is a typical Perpendicular church but was built only in 1829-31 with

great antiquarian accuracy. The George Inn, formerly on the other side of the road, was once famous as a coaching inn. John Byng in 1789 found it a 'Tolerable Noon Stop' with beef steak for 8d and beer 3d. At the southern end of the village, beyond the commendable Star and Garter, is Silsoe College, part of Cranfield University. Historic Wrest Park is occupied by the Silsoe Research Institute.

Wrest Park, page 34.

Slip End

Woodside Farm and Wildlife Park, page 100.

Southill

In this pleasing estate village almost every house bears a Whitbread monogram. Samuel Whitbread (the first) bought the estate in 1795 from the Byng family. He died the following year and his son Samuel (the second) moved to Southill House and had it modernised and embellished by Henry Holland. Christopher Hussey has written: 'Southill must be acknowledged the classic example of the most civilised decade in the whole range of English domestic architecture.' For Pevsner

'Southill is one of the most exquisite English understatements'. The house is not open to the public, though the gardens by 'Capability' Brown are opened occasionally.

Church of All Saints, page 78.

Stagsden

Recently bypassed, this is a village of the uplands between the Ouse and the Ouzel which extend to the edge of Milton Keynes and are a prelude to the somewhat anonymous country that does not vary till beyond Buckingham. The core of the village has a lot of thatch and a pleasing sense of enclosure. It was here, in March 1270, that ten-year-old William Stil dropped a knife on his foot and bled to death in his mother's arms. On a central island dominating the village stands St Lawrence's church. The lower part of the tower is thirteenth-century, as is the south doorway, and perhaps the north wall of the nave and chancel. The south aisle was added early in the fourteenth century when the south wall of the church was rebuilt. The square font is of the same date and has later figures of a man and woman cut into it. The screen dates from the fifteenth century. There is a brass of John Cocke and his daughter (both died 1617).

Staploe

In spring the road from Bushmead to Upper Staploe is a delight with planted daffodils, but in June roadside nature reserves between Begwary, Honeydon and Upper Staploe provide a habitat for the rare spiked star of Bethlehem, sulphur clover and crested cow-wheat. Staploe is a small hamlet of yellow brick and recent infill. There is an old gospel hall and sixteenth-century Topham's Farm, but the Three Horseshoes is no more.

Water in the Duloe brook, which runs along the main street, is too low to show to advantage.

Duloe has one or two thatched cottages, and in Woodhouse Lane an overgrown eighteenth-century dovecote in disrepair, built with attractive red bricks and roofed in warm mottled tiles. Basmead Manor, once the home of the Wauton family, is a beautifully restored timbered building originating in the fourteenth

century, and almost surrounded by a moat.

Honeydon has a tiny Methodist chapel built in 1872. This is not surprising, perhaps, because here was born Mary Fielding, a Methodist who emigrated to America and married Hyrum Smith, the Mormon leader. She luckily escaped the massacre in which her husband was murdered and struggled across America for four years with four wagons to reach Salt Lake City. There she died in 1852.

Stevington

In the centre of this beautiful limestone village stands the medieval market cross, restored in the mid nineteenth century. East of the village is the restored windmill, built for Richard Pool about 1770. At West End is a dignified Baptist church built in 1720, with quiet interior and tiny graveyard at the front.

Church of St Mary, page 78; **Stevington Post Mill**, page 87.

Stondon

Transport Museum and Garden Centre, page 96.

Stotfold

Stotfold fits into the south-eastern corner of the county, only a mile from its big Hertfordshire neighbour, Letchworth. Although it is an old settlement (its name meaning 'an enclosure for stud horses' can be traced back to *Stodfald* in 1007), today one has to search for the old village. Off the main road, it lies to the north around St Mary's church and Stotfold Green.

The fire-damaged watermill and Stotfoldbury make a pleasant corner, and the Church Almshouses in Mill Lane 'for poor widows and married couples who are fifty years of age', should be noted. Look out for Tithe Cottage and the Regency period vicarage. The Cage or village lock-up is on the corner of Rook Tree Lane and Queen's Street. A plaque facing into the churchyard marks the Boys' School erected by Henricus Octavus Roe in 1808. Roe was the son of a vicar of Stotfold and endowed the village with numerous generous charities before he died in 1854.

In 1830 Stotfold was the scene of the Bread Riots, brought about by high prices, low

The Baptist church in Stevington.

wages and unemployment. Farms were picketed and shops pilfered. The vicar of Hinxworth (Hertfordshire) considered that a major uprising was imminent and, together with a local justice, assembled 120 special constables and arrested ten of the ringleaders, three of whom were transported.

At the southern end of the parish the vast yellow brick Fairfield Hospital, designed by G. F. Jones in 1857 and frequently extended, has provided employment for many local people but is now scheduled for closure in 1997.

Streatley
Galley Hill, page 50.

Sutton
This street village has a few good old houses with sagging tiled roofs and scalloped Victorian bargeboards. A ford and fourteenth-century packhorse bridge cross a narrow tributary of the river Ivel. The Old Rectory dates from about 1550 and is timber-framed and plastered. Beside it stands All Saints' church.

Church of All Saints, page 79.

Swineshead
The village street is particularly pleasing when viewed from the east with Three Horseshoes Cottage and School House catching the eye, and the high slender limestone spire of St Nicholas's church crowning the scene. Moat Farm beside the church is a seventeenth-century brown-washed timber-framed building, once the rectory. When it was being restored in 1864 a copy of the Solemn League and Covenant (against the use of Archbishop Laud's Prayer Book) was discovered in the roof, signed by the vicar of Swineshead and cautiously hidden. Most of the church dates from the fourteenth century. It has a painted fifteenth-century rood screen and chancel stalls with misericords of the same date. A frieze of heads and ballflowers runs below the parapet outside the church.

Opposite: All Saints' church, Shillington, and the former school. The church bells are said to have rolled down the hill into the stream when the tower collapsed in 1701.

Tebworth

This small hamlet in Chalgrave parish is somewhat larger than its parent. It is well worth a detour. Along the main road are a number of buildings in red and blue chequered brick patterns, such as Tithe Farm, with its massive chimney stack, and Buttercup Farm with timber-framing and thatch. Especially notable in The Lane are number 2 and Emmertones Cottage, both with timber and thatch. Hidden in Wingfield Road is the surprising Shoulder of Mutton Cottage, formerly an inn. In **Wingfield** itself is Pond Farm, dated 1699, with timber-frame and brick nogging.

Tempsford

Tempsford is a quiet little village split by the A1. In the northern section are four thatched cottages, as well as some of timber and daub construction. A mile to the east was RAF Tempsford Airfield, the base from which the Special Operations Executive dropped equipment and secret agents into German-occupied Europe during the Second World War. Church End is a particularly attractive area. Notable are Church Farm (restored 1775) and Gannock House with the Wheatsheaf Inn opposite (both seventeenth-century). Gannock's Castle is a small medieval moated site.
Church of St Peter, page 79.

Thurleigh

Thurleigh is a very attractive village, with plenty of timber framing and thatch in the main street beside the church. The large Norman castle mound is overgrown and uncared for. It was once the home of Hugh de Lega. There is the tower of a disused windmill west of the village, and there are pleasing old buildings at Scald End, a name derived from a 'school' set up by the Francklins of Bolnhurst in 1618.
Church of St Peter, page 79.

Tilsworth

This tiny village has three architectural treasures. Manor Farm gatehouse, built of ironstone in the fifteenth century, once gave access across a moat to the home of the Chamberlain family. At the rear of Granary Farm is a superb timber and orange brick medieval barn, visible from the road. The third treasure is the church of All Saints.
Church of All Saints, page 79.

Conservation at its best in the quiet village of Swineshead.

Black and white, chequer-board and stripes at Tempsford.

Toddington

The houses round the green are a delight to enthusiasts of vernacular architecture: in particular Conger Cottage, Villa and House at the entrance to Conger Lane, and the seventeenth-century Wentworth House built in the chequered-brick style of central Bedfordshire. The Oddfellows Arms and the Sow and Pigs are but two of numerous popular public houses, the latter the unlikely venue of a flourishing poetry-reading society. Toddington Manor, built about 1570, is only a fragment of the much larger mansion in which lived Henrietta Wentworth, mistress of the Duke of Monmouth.

In **Chalton** to the south look out for the fine half-timbered Gostelow House of 1540, surrounded by a web of electricity cables and pylons.

Church of St George, page 79; **Conger Hill**, page 60; **Shrove Tuesday ceremony**, page 108; **Toddington Manor Rare Breeds Centre**, page 98.

In the locality: churches at Chalgrave, page 65; and Harlington, page 69.

Totternhoe

Totternhoe is divided into three parts. Much of the village lies below the spur of Castle Hill. To the south cluster numerous old houses around Church End, and at the north is a mainly modern settlement at Lower End. Castle Hill dominates the village. Below, the Cross Keys Inn is one of a number of timbered and thatched buildings scattered through the village. Most of these are at Church End, which is well worth an extended visit, especially in apple-blossom time. St Giles's church was built of the local Totternhoe stone in the fourteenth century, on the site of an earlier building. Its east window is a Tree of Life by John Piper and Patrick Reyntiens (1970). On its exterior walls are numerous fragile graffiti, of medieval post mills, possibly drawn as late as the eighteenth century. Under the field southeast of the church the remains of a Roman courtyard villa lie buried. Doolittle Mill combined a tower windmill and watermill but was wrecked by a storm and ceased working in 1880.

Doolittle Mill at Totternhoe.

Totternhoe Castle and quarries, page 62; **Totternhoe Knolls**, page 58.

Turvey

This is a delightful nineteenth-century limestone estate village, spoilt only by the busy A428. The Ouse forms the county boundary, crossed by a bridge mainly of 1795. Two statues in the river are mere curiosities, one nicknamed Jonah acquired from Ashridge, Hertfordshire, in 1844, and the other with female body and male head set up in 1953. On the wall of the Three Fyshes floods of 1797, 1823 and 1947 are recorded. For addicts of the vernacular Turvey is a joy, ranging from 'Gothic' Richmond House to the mock ecclesiastical Chantry Farm buildings. Barncroft leads to Vine Cottage, still with vine, 'built by W. Bithrey 1823'. There are attractive groups of cottages at the corner of Newton Lane and in Abbey Square opposite Jack's Lane. Turvey Abbey is a Jaco-

Opposite: *High Street, Silsoe.*

bean house used since 1980 as a Benedictine monastery for monks and nuns.
Church of All Saints, page 80.

Upper Dean
See under Dean, page 16.

Upper Gravenhurst
See under Gravenhurst, page 21.

Upper Sundon
Sundon Hills Country Park, page 58.

Westoning

About the year 1200 Eilward of Westoning brawled with his neighbour Fulk over a 2d debt and struck him severely with a whetstone. Arrested, tried and found guilty at Leighton Buzzard, Eilward's eyes were put out and he was castrated. Later, as he prayed for forgiveness, St Thomas of Canterbury appeared in a vision and his sight and mutilations were restored. This odd story is illustrated in a window in Canterbury Cathedral.

St Mary's church is mostly fourteenth-century with a fifteenth-century tower and spire. The font is earlier, perhaps thirteenth-century. Opposite the church is The Grange, a timber-framed building with orange brick nogging. The Manor of 1843 is now a Macintyre Home for Handicapped Children. Inside there is woodwork from Wrest Park and the Palace of Westminster. At the cross-roads is the thatched Chequers Inn, fortunately spared when a petrol lorry exploded in the village in September 1976, destroying a number of buildings.

Whipsnade

Whipsnade has an extensive undulating village green, with pleasant, mainly modern houses around its edge. Gates at each end used to close the road at night. A brick tower of the sixteenth century and an eighteenth-century nave make St Mary's the only brick church in the county older than the nineteenth century. There is an unusual apsidal chancel of 1866. A National Trust signpost on the green directs visitors to Tree Cathedral, an area of 20 acres (8 hectares) planted with twenty-five species of trees, in the approximate plan of a cathedral, devised in 1930 by E. K. Blyth as a living memorial to friends killed in the First World War. In front of Dell Farm a bridleway leads north on to a little-used section of the Whipsnade Downs owned by the National Trust (also car park at Bison Hill; OS 165: SP 999185), where panoramic views are particularly fine.

Dunstable and Whipsnade Downs, page 50; **Whipsnade Wild Animal Park**, page 98.

Willington

Willington Dovecote and Stables, page 88.

Wingfield

See under Tebworth, page 38.

Woburn

Woburn is a beautifully preserved Georgian village with fine eighteenth-century houses along the High Street and Bedford Street. Glimpses of the backs tell us that many are of medieval origin. The old school next to old St Mary's church originated in Elizabethan times and has been used for education from 1582 until the present. The village suffered a number of disastrous fires, the first in 1595 when an old woman, 'as simple and silly as ever I knew', threw her bed straw into the fireplace and succeeded in burning down 130 houses. Others in 1645 burnt twenty-seven houses, and in 1724 destroyed thirty-nine. Most of the buildings date from the rebuilding after the last event. Some, such as 17 Bedford Street and the Clifford Gallery, have curled doorcase columns believed to be unique to Bedfordshire. At the north end of Bedford Street are two ranges of yellow brick almshouses with stepped gables of 1850. The village caters for tourists and is filled with restaurants and antique shops, as well as a Heritage Centre.

Church of St Mary, page 80; **Woburn Abbey**, page 90; **Woburn Heritage Centre**, page 96; **Woburn Safari Park**, page 99.

In the locality: Segenhoe Old Church, page 86; and churches at Aspley Guise, page 63; Battlesden, page 63; Eversholt, page 68; Milton Bryan, page 74; and Potsgrove, page 76.

Wrestlingworth

Trees are a feature of this village, hiding a number of mediocre buildings and framing some of the more interesting ones. The Chequers Inn is a pleasant timber and plaster seventeenth-century building. Elsewhere in the High Street, Home Farmhouse and Hill Farmhouse, both of about the same date, are worth seeking out. Past the council houses and around the church and school are pleasing individual buildings, especially the thatched Ivy Cottage, dated 1829, and Jasmine Cottage of 1851. The Lower School has been happily designed and lies snug beneath its protective chestnut tree.

In 1843 Sarah Dazley of Wrestlingworth was executed for poisoning her husband with arsenic. Aged twenty-four, she was the last woman to be publicly hanged outside Bedford jail, an event avidly watched by most of her fellow villagers, though clearly repugnant to the prison chaplain, for whom 'no tongue can tell, or pen describe, the anxiety

Fine Georgian façades in the centre of Woburn.

and distress I endure on those awful occasions'.

St Peter's church has been ruthlessly restored, though a few traces of early work are still visible. The west gallery and box pews remain from the early Victorian period. South of the church are a fine group of late seventeenth-century tombstones.

Yelden

Church of St Mary, page 80;
Yielden Castle, page 62.

Sutton packhorse bridge.

Opposite: *Sharpenhoe Clapper and the village.*

Willington dovecote.

3
The countryside

The county of Bedford came into existence in Saxon times, and the first recorded mention of it is in the Anglo-Saxon Chronicle for the year 1011, soon after the Danes had ravaged Bedford. The boundary only approximately corresponds to that in use today. It is one of the smallest counties, largely given over to agriculture, with an area of 477 square miles (123,563 hectares).

The geological map of Bedfordshire looks like a rugby jersey with formations crossing the county in a series of bands, with the youngest rocks in the south and the oldest in the north-west. These are chalk, gault clay, lower greensand with pockets of Ampthill and Kimmeridge clay, Oxford clay and finally oolitic limestone. Superimposed on this 'solid' geology are the clays and gravels deposited by glaciers during the various ice ages. These range from clay-with-flints overlying the chalk in the extreme south to patches of glacial gravel and vast areas of boulder clay that cover much of the central and northern parts of the county.

A major river, the Great Ouse, with its tributaries the Ivel and Ouzel, winds its way across the county, giving additional deposits of river gravel and alluvium. The Lea rises at Leagrave and runs south through a misfit valley in the Chilterns to join the Thames at Canning Town.

This complex mixture of deposits gives rise to soils of widely differing characteristics, from light and dry to heavy and wet, and from acid to highly alkaline. All have their own flora and fauna.

Some soils, like the river gravel around Biggleswade and Sandy, are very fertile and market gardening flourishes to the exclusion of wildlife habitats. Aerial photography and excavation show that they once proved popular for prehistoric human settlement.

The heavy clay soils were mostly run-down permanent pasture until the Second World War, but the majority are now under cereals and oilseed rape. Only one or two old pastures remain with their abundant flowers, and these are vulnerable to agricultural improvement. Fortunately a number of fine woodlands still stand on the clay.

The greensand is much less fertile, and the characteristic vegetation is heather and bracken. It is well wooded, and there are extensive conifer plantations.

The chalk downs, part of the Chilterns Area of Outstanding Natural Beauty, form the most dramatic landscape in the county. What were once sheep-grazed downs are now great arable fields. Some wild areas do remain, mostly in steep dry valleys, old quarries and road and railway cuttings. The loss of the sheep and the enormous reduction of the rabbit population by myxomatosis in the 1950s have allowed bushes, especially hawthorn and dog rose, to spread over the chalk grassland. It was these well-drained chalk hills that were particularly favoured by prehistoric man for settlement, and many of the best-preserved archaeological sites are to be found in this area.

Gravel, clay, sand and chalk have all proved attractive for mineral exploitation. Gravel extraction plants are to be found along the Ouse and Ivel valleys, while at Leighton Buzzard sand is excavated in vast quantities, and rare fuller's earth at Aspley Heath. On the clay at Stewartby was, until recently, the world's largest brickworks, and in the south around Totternhoe and Dunstable are vast chalk quarries.

The many disused man-made pits make some of the most exciting wildlife habitats in the county. Gravel pits teem with dragonflies in the summer and form a haven for waterfowl in the winter. Some have now become nature reserves. The largest pits in Bedfordshire are in the Marston Vale, south of Bedford, where giant excavators dig clay for the famous Fletton bricks. Some old claypits have become sailing lakes, while others remain as 'moonscapes', where nature is undisturbed. So, while many of the former wetlands and marshes have been drained and disappear under the plough, some of their flora and fauna have been able to colonise the new watery habitats. It has been claimed that there is now more water in the county than at any time since natural history observations began.

The geology of the county is reflected in the architecture. The clay has produced bricks and tiles since the fifteenth century, often of warm orange, red and grey in the south and pale yellow further north. Occasionally flint, too, is used for building in the south. From the chalk comes the mortar which bonds them, as well as the Totternhoe stone familiar in half the county's churches. The oolitic limestone in the north-west gives us the warm cream-coloured buildings characteristic of the upper Ouse and Nene valleys, and sandstone and cobbles have created the rusty stone churches of mid Bedfordshire. Everywhere trees provided timber for beams and roofs, and cornfields and riverbanks the straw and reeds for thatch.

In addition to the nature reserves described here, there are several smaller reserves, owned or managed by the Wildlife Trust. Details of membership are available from the Trust in Priory Park, Bedford (telephone: 01234 64213).

Ampthill Park, Ampthill (car park, OS 153: TL 024382).

Ampthill Castle was built by Sir John Cornwall on a hill to the west of the town early in the fifteenth century. In 1508 it became the property of Henry VII and was popular with his son Henry VIII, who placed it at the disposal of Katharine of Aragon whilst her divorce was pending. Later it fell into ruins, and the present house was built on a new site by Lord Ashburnham after 1697, using various architects including Hawksmoor, Lumley, Winde and perhaps Archer. The park was landscaped by 'Capability' Brown about 1770 for Lord Ossory, who, at Horace Walpole's suggestion, set up the Gothic cross on the site of the castle in memory of Katharine of Aragon. The park now forms an attractive open space ideal for walking and fishing, with facilities for football, cricket, tennis and cross-country running. Most is rough grassland, grazed by cattle, with groves of birch trees and drifts of gorse, pignut, heath

Katharine's Cross in Ampthill Park.

bedstraw, wavy hair-grass, lesser stitchwort, tormentil and harebells – all plants that thrive on acid soils. Scattered throughout are groups of splendid specimen trees (oak, Scots pine, beech, lime, sweet chestnut and sycamore) and on the east side of the park is a plantation, largely of sycamore, carpeted with bluebells in spring. A large shallow lake, partly covered with fringed water-lily, adds further wildlife interest to the site, as do several small marshes. Characteristic birds are yellow, hammers and willow warblers. The park is interesting to visit throughout the year.

Bradger's Hill, Luton (car park, OS166: TL 092245). Park at John Dony Field Centre, Hancock Drive, Bushmead. Telephone: 01582 486983. The centre has leaflets, displays and a teaching laboratory and materials and is open on weekdays and Sunday mornings. Toilets.

Bradger's Hill is a steep chalk escarpment within a few minutes walk of the field centre with well-marked paths and a nature trail with numbered posts. The slope faces northwest and there are fine views over Luton from the top. In Saxon times, and probably much earlier, a parallel series of cultivation terraces was formed on the hillside. These are called strip lynchets. Old photographs show that some of them were still under the plough as late as the 1920s. Now these strips are grassland kept open by grazing or mowing and have characteristic chalk flowers such as rockrose, wild thyme, milkwort, cowslips, yellow-wort, pyramidal and spotted orchids and autumn gentians. Scrub has invaded the slopes (or risers) between the terraces, in places shading out the grass completely. The bushes are mostly of hawthorn and dogwood but a few bird-sown garden shrubs are present from the nearby housing estate and young yew trees from the specimens in Stopsley churchyard. The shelter provided by the scrub makes the grassy terraces ideal for butterflies. There is a good colony of the small blue as well as marbled whites and various skippers. The best time to visit Bradger's Hill is from April to

Opposite: *Ampthill House from Ampthill Park.*

October and stout footwear should be worn as the chalk can be slippery.

Bramingham Wood, Luton (main entrance, OS 166: TL 072255). The Woodland Trust. Park cars at the end of Lygetun Drive adjacent to the wood. For Woodland Trust membership details telephone 01476 74297.

Now surrounded by housing estates and school playing fields, this fine wood is one of the Woodland Trust's Community Woodlands, managed by local volunteers. It was originally two woods separated by a narrow strip. The southern tip is fenced off for use by Scouts and Guides but the rest of the wood is open to the public and has numerous paths and entrances. Large oaks, ashes, field maples and crab apples form the canopy, with a shrub layer mostly of hazel, coppiced on a fifteen-year rotation. Much of the woodland floor is covered with bramble enlivened with spring flowers such as red campion, bluebells, yellow archangel and wood avens. The bird life is surprisingly rich and grey squirrels are abundant and unafraid. The wood is interesting at all times of year but wellington boots may be essential in winter.

Brogborough Hill Picnic Site, Brogborough (OS 153: SP 965387). Bedfordshire County Council.

This site adjoins the A421 Bedford to M1 link road. It is an extensive hilltop with wide views over Marston Vale and the Bedfordshire brickfields. There are toilets.

Bromham Mill Picnic Site, Bromham (OS 153: TL 011507). Bedfordshire County Council.

At the west end of Bromham bridge, this is a large riverside picnic site beside the Ouse, with plenty of wildlife. There are toilets.

Centenary Wood, Pulloxhill (entrance, OS153: TL 062351). Bedfordshire County Council. Leaflet available from the County Council Planning Department.

This 34 acre (14 hectare) site was arable until 1989, when it was planted with thousands of trees and shrubs, both native and non-native, to commemorate the County

Council's centenary. The plan is to develop a landscape feature where the public and school parties are welcome. Ponds have already been dug and new hedges planted to link with existing ones which will be allowed to spread to form thickets. The new wood will be managed in a variety of ways with part coppiced and part growing unchecked. A central area is to become a grazed parkland.

Chicksands Wood, Shefford (OS 153: TL 106411). Forestry Commission.

This is a large wood mostly on ill-drained clay with wide rides full of butterflies in summer. Originally a mixed deciduous wood, it is now partly replanted with spruce, Thuya and Corsican pine, but some interesting trees such as small-leaved lime and hornbeam remain, and many trees are hung with traveller's joy. Ground flora includes primroses, wood spurge, bluebells, bugle and yellow archangel under the trees, with bush vetch, bird's-foot trefoil and lesser stitchwort a feature of the rides, as well as patches of ragged robin, meadowsweet and common knapweed. Chinese muntjac deer are abundant. The best time to visit is between April and October.

Cooper's Hill, Ampthill (OS 153: TL 028376). Managed by the Wildlife Trust for Ampthill Town Council.

This is a low hill on the greensand, covered with heather, bracken, gorse, broom, birch and scrubby oaks. Until 1770 it was a rabbit warren, and from 1842 until 1917 a pine plantation. The pines were felled during the First World War and not replanted, giving a chance for heather growing on the rides to colonise the whole site. Cooper's Hill is famous for its unusual sand-loving insects. Parts are on a spring line and form a wet acid 'mire', with interesting plants such as skullcap and great horsetail. Tree pipits sing from the birches, which may hold flocks of redpolls in the autumn. The best time to visit is between April and October.

Dallow Downs, Luton (entrance, OS 166: TL 072217). Park in Runley Road. Luton Borough Council. Leaflet available from Luton Museum (telephone: 01582 36941) and John

Dony Field Centre (telephone: 01582 486983).

Dallow Downs is a surprisingly large area of chalk downland in the south-west corner of Luton, skirted by the M1 and surrounded by houses and factories. Several roads give access, one bisecting the site, and tarmacked paths connect them. The steep hillside is partly covered by hawthorn and dogwood scrub of various ages, grading into woodland, but there are still open patches of chalk grassland with its characteristic flora. Local conservation groups cut some of the young scrub to preserve the grassland as grazing is not feasible. Strip lynchets are present in one wooded area, indicating pre-Roman terrace cultivation. The best time to visit is from April to October. The steep paths can be very muddy and slippery and it is advisable to wear boots.

Deadman's Hill Picnic Site, Clophill (OS 153: TL 073394). Bedfordshire County Council.

One mile (1.6 km) north of Clophill, on the west side of the A6 at the summit of Deadman's Hill, this site is attractive in summer with flowers typical of clay grasslands and has access to Maulden Wood (see page 55). The name of the site has nothing to do with the 'A6 murder', which took place here in 1961, for which James Hanratty was executed in Bedford prison the following year.

Dunstable and Whipsnade Downs, Dunstable (car parks, OS 165: TL 007178 and SP 998186). Bedfordshire County Council and National Trust. Countryside Centre: telephone 01582 608489. Leaflet available. Toilets on Dunstable Downs.

This is the largest stretch of chalk downland in the county, and the Dunstable end is in danger of being over-visited. The chalk flora has suffered from scrub invasion, and in some areas from excessive trampling, but many characteristic flowers can still be found, such as fairy flax, kidney vetch, clustered bellflower, harebell, dropwort, thyme, small scabious and squinancywort. Butterflies include colonies of the chalk hill blue and the small blue. The triangulation point is the highest in Bedfordshire (243 metres, 797 feet),

The chalk downs at Whipsnade, looking towards Dunstable.

and there are tremendous views west over the Vale of Aylesbury. The best time to visit is from May to October.

Felmersham Gravel Pits, Felmersham (car park, OS 153: SP 987583). The Wildlife Trust.

These disused gravel workings, covering 52 acres (21 hectares) near the river Ouse, are now a Site of Special Scientific Interest and a nature reserve. The gravel was dug to make concrete for aerodrome runways during the Second World War. The pits are mostly shallow with ridges of spoil forming spits and islands, some colonised by willows. As well as open water, teeming with dragonflies in the summer, there are marshy areas, meadows, scrub and developing woodland. The reserve is interesting throughout the year.

Flitwick Moor, Flitwick (car park, OS 153: TL 046354). From Maulden Road, track beside Folly Farm. The Wildlife Trust.

This 79 acre (32 hectare) nature reserve is unique in the county. Part is rough pasture, usually grazed by cattle, but most of the site is old peat workings. Please keep to the footpaths as peat habitats are easily damaged by

trampling. The peat was originally cut for fuel for the poor of local parishes, and more recently, until 1967, for use in removing impurities during the manufacture of coal gas. Now the shallow diggings have been colonised by vegetation forming a range of habitats including sphagnum bog, marshy areas with moisture-loving plants such as meadowsweet, comfrey and marsh-marigold, and pools filled with reeds, bulrushes and various sedges. Alders and willows are established in the wet areas, while the drier parts have become open woodland of birch and oak. In the northern half of the reserve iron-rich chalybeate springs turn the water in the ditches bright orange. This water was bottled and fraudulently sold as a tonic in the late nineteenth and early twentieth centuries.

Flitwick Wood, Flitwick (entrances off Byron Crescent or Manor Way, OS 153: TL 025350 and TL 024351). Bedfordshire County Council owns the eastern half of the wood, the rest is owned privately. Leaflet available from the County Council Planning Department.

This attractive wood adjoins the west edge of the village. Most of Flitwick Wood is an excellent example of a well-managed ancient wood on a heavy boulder-clay soil. There are widely spaced standard trees of oak and ash with actively coppiced hazel underneath, as well as patches of blackthorn and guelder-rose. Poplars in the eastern corner, planted in the 1940s, are being felled and replaced with oaks. Much of the wood floor is covered with tussocks of the delicate tufted hair-grass but there are also typical woodland flowers such as bluebells, primroses, dog's mercury and wood spurge. Chinese muntjac deer abound. Parts of the wood are wet in winter and wellington boots should be worn.

Forty Foot Lane Picnic Site, Harrold (OS 153: SP 932597). Bedfordshire County Council.

On the east side of the Harrold to Hinwick road, about halfway between the two villages, this is a quiet site in a mixed plantation offering a number of short walks.

Galley and Warden Hills, Luton (car park, OS 166: TL 085259). Luton Borough Council. Local Nature Reserve. Site of Special Scientific Interest. Park in lay-by adjacent to golf course, by Cardinal Newman School entrance. Information board near lay-by and leaflets available from Luton Museum, Wardown Park, and John Dony Field Centre (see page 94 and also under Bradger's Hill, page 49).

These twin chalk hills adjoin the north-east corner of Luton and give marvellous views over the town from their upper slopes. On their west side they are flanked by a golf course and the ancient Icknield Way, now a green lane. Following the outbreak of myxomatosis in the mid 1950s the hills became covered with scrub. Now much has been cleared by volunteers but scattered bushes have been retained and a few thickets. Hawthorn dominates but buckthorn and wayfaring-tree are also common in places with occasional dogwood, wild privet, dog rose and elder. The sward is variable but there are still many areas of flower-rich turf, alive with butterflies in summer. The Wildlife Trust, which manages the site, has recently reintroduced sheep grazing after a gap of nearly fifty

years. This should encourage the chalkland flowers such as rock-rose, cowslips, kidney and horseshoe vetch, orchids and gentians. These low hills are used by migrating birds in spring and autumn, especially wheatears, pipits and warblers, and in winter visitors may be lucky enough to see a harrier or a short-eared owl hunting over the grass. Hares are abundant and foxes and muntjac deer lie up in the thickets. The site is of interest throughout the year. Chalk can be very slippery and it is sensible to wear boots.

The Greensand Ridge Walk

This 40 mile (64 km) footpath follows the greensand outcrop of mid Bedfordshire and was inaugurated by the County Council in October 1986. It consists of many public footpaths and short stretches of road and is well signposted with muntjac deer emblems on all posts. Even so, the route is complicated and copies of the guide map should be obtained from Leisure Services, Bedfordshire County Council, County Hall, Bedford (telephone 01234 228310) or local tourist information centres and libraries.

The footpath follows the Grand Union Canal towpath north from Leighton Buzzard to the Globe public house, then leads round Stockgrove Country Park to Woburn. It proceeds through the Deer Park to Eversholt, north to Jackdaw Hill, Lidlington, and on to Ampthill Park and Houghton House. The walk continues through Maulden, Clophill, Northill and Beeston to Sandy, and then follows a Roman road to Everton, finishing just over the county boundary at Gamlingay Cinques in Cambridgeshire. Six short circular walks have also been set up in conjunction with the main walk. Details are available from the Leisure Services department.

Harrold-Odell Country Park, Harrold (car park, OS 153: SP 960568). Bedfordshire County Council. Visitor centre, leaflet, toilets. Telephone: 01234 720016.

This is an area of 144 acres (58 hectares) of former gravel workings and water meadows on the north side of the Great Ouse. It is ideal for walking, with several paths to follow. There is a large lake attractive to waterfowl in

The Harrold-Odell Country Park, looking towards Chellington.

the winter, with a central island kept partly clear of vegetation to encourage the nesting of common terns, lapwings, redshanks and little ringed plovers. Flocks of feral greylag and Canada geese roost on the lake and graze on the grasslands. The former gravel-washing area is now a nature sanctuary, with a central gravelly ridge, surrounded by willow carr, marshes and pools. The ridge is bright with tufted vetch and tall melilot in summer, and in the autumn stands of teasels and thistles attract goldfinches and peacock butterflies.

The marsh is carpeted with marsh horsetail and there are patches of ragged robin, purple loosestrife, wild angelica and greater bird's-foot trefoil and dense thickets of sallows and osiers. The river is fringed with water-plantain and great yellow-cress. The country park is interesting to visit throughout the year, but peak numbers of birds are present in January and February.

Holcot Wood and Woodland Creation Scheme, Brogborough (entrance, OS 153: SP 966388). Park at the adjacent Brogborough Picnic Site, which is off the A421. The Woodland Trust.

Holcot Wood can be reached from the picnic-site access road by taking the bridleway past Brogborough Manor Farm. It is part of a large area purchased by the Woodland Trust in 1992. The wood itself is most attractive and is situated on a ridge with fine views over the Marston Vale. Like many old Bedfordshire woods on a heavy clay soil, the standard trees are oak and ash, with ancient coppice stools of ash, maple and hazel. A large central glade has two ponds. There are more ponds scattered over the rest of the 241 acre (98 hectare) site, most of which consists of new plantations of ash, maple, oak and wild cherry with a wide variety of woodland shrubs. The strip adjacent to Holcot Wood is being allowed to regenerate naturally and the slopes below will form an extensive new meadow.

110 yards (100 metres) further north-east along the picnic-site access road is the entrance to the 'Woodland Creation' area, where there is a Woodland Trust sign and information board. This Woodland Trust site is part of the Marston Vale Community Forest, an ambitious project covering over 60 square miles (160 square km) south of Bedford, in a part of the county blighted by the brickmaking industry. The project aims to increase tree cover from the present 5 per cent of the area to 35 per cent by the year 2020. Holcot Wood and the Woodland Creation Scheme are interesting throughout the year. Wellington boots are usually essential.

Icknield Way Path

This footpath links the Ridgeway Path at Ivinghoe, Buckinghamshire, with the Peddars Way Path in Norfolk. Historically the Bedfordshire section ran in roughly a straight line from Dunstable Downs to Deacon Hill at Pegsdon, but, in order to avoid most of the built-up area of Dunstable and Luton, the officially designated path deviates somewhat from that line. It is easiest to join the Bedfordshire section at the National Trust's Bison Hill car park (OS 165: TL 999185) at Whipsnade. The path proceeds east along the Whipsnade and Dunstable Downs and crosses the golf course before passing through Dunstable and east on to Blow's Downs. After it crosses the M1 motorway, it follows roads and paths north past the Challney High Schools to Leagrave railway station and Bramingham Road. Here it follows the River Lea Walk for a while before heading northeast to Weybourne Drive and on to Warden Hill. From the summit of the hill the path runs north to Galley Hill and on to the traditional course of the Icknield Way as marked on Ordnance Survey sheet 166. It continues east to Telegraph Hill (Hertfordshire) and back into Bedfordshire above Pegsdon, before heading for Pirton in Hertfordshire. Detailed maps and directions can be found in the Icknield Way Association's excellent book *The Icknield Way Path: A Walkers' Guide* (1993) available from the Membership Secretary, 19 Boundary Road, Bishop's Stortford, Hertfordshire CM23 5LE (telephone: 01279 504602), or good bookshops.

Kingswood and Glebe Meadows, Houghton Conquest (car park for Houghton House, OS 153: TL 038393). Bedfordshire County Council.

Kingswood is an ancient oak, ash and maple woodland with some elm (mostly dead) and a few planted limes, sycamores and hornbeams. It lies on the north slope of the greensand ridge, overlooking the claypits of the Marston Vale, but the soil is mostly ill-drained boulder clay, with only a few pockets of greensand. Bluebells, yellow archangel, wood anemones and pendulous sedge cover the wood floor, with ferns in the shadier parts.

The best time to visit is April to June. Wellington boots should be worn.

The Glebe Meadows, north of the wood, are three old pastures on clay soil, now part grazed and part cut for hay. Cowslips, buttercups, restharrow, knapweed and sawwort make these meadows colourful from May to October. An old field pond favoured by frogs and thick overgrown hedges add to the wildlife interest.

The Lodge, Sandy (car park, OS 153: TL 191485). Access from B1042, Sandy to Potton road. The headquarters of the Royal Society for the Protection of Birds. Telephone: 01767 680541.

The house called The Lodge was built for Viscount Peel in 1890, designed by the architect Henry Clutton. The grounds consist of 106 acres (43 hectares) of gardens (open to the public), mixed woodland, an artificial lake, a disused quarry and a relict area of heathland, a habitat that used to be more commonly found along the greensand ridge. There are several trails and hides with facilities suitable for the disabled. There is a gift shop and information point with toilets and a picnic area adjacent to the car park.

In common with most woodland, the reserve is at its best throughout spring and early summer when the birds are easier to see, singing out their territorial boundaries over a carpet of daffodils, then bluebells, followed by the flowering of rhododendrons. Of the fifty recorded breeding species of birds, the majority nest in the woodland. Woodcock, nuthatch, treecreeper and all three woodpecker species may be found here, along with muntjac deer, yellow-necked mouse and five species of bat. Many different species of fungi may be found throughout the autumn. Look out for the mixed flocks of tits and other resident birds that rove through the woods in winter. Some of these frequent the lake to drink, bathe and feed at the bird tables overlooked by a hide suitable for wheelchair users.

Much of the work on the reserve is aimed at managing the heather on the existing heathland, a nationally rare habitat and the second largest example in the county, and extending this habitat into the adjacent pine plantation for the benefit of native wildlife. This includes the successfully reintroduced population of natterjack toads, which can now be found naturally on only two inland heathland sites in Britain. Rabbits abound both here and on the meadow adjacent the lake.

Marston Thrift, Wood End, Marston Moretaine (car park, OS 153: SP 973412). Bedfordshire County Council.

Marston Thrift is a 140 acre (56.4 hectare) area of woodland on boulder clay situated on a south-facing slope between Cranfield and Marston. The lower and wetter part, extending over 80 acres (32.3 hectares), is ancient woodland consisting of oak, ash and field maple, with hazel coppice and blackthorn. The remaining 60 acres (24.1 hectares) were replanted with conifers in 1962 and 1972. Records of the Thrift date back to 1287, and coppicing appears to have been carried out continuously from medieval times until 1945. Since 1974 areas of the ancient woodland have been coppiced. Pendulous sedge grows in the wetter parts of the Thrift, which also feature yellow archangel, bugle, bluebell, primrose and small teasel. Visitors may see muntjac, fox, squirrel, all three woodpeckers, tawny owl, nuthatch, various tits, goldcrest and a wide variety of butterflies and moths. One area of the higher ground is planted with Lawson cypress and western red cedar, the other with Norway and Omorika spruce and Corsican pine. On parts of the highest ground the conifers have died back and deciduous regrowth has taken place; these areas feature privet, dog's mercury and spurges. Near the centre of the Thrift, in a section of Corsican pine, the County Council has dug two ponds, which have been allowed to colonise naturally since being excavated in 1988. The Thrift is attractive all year round, but at most times wellington boots are essential. It is not suitable for wheelchairs.

Maulden Wood, Maulden (car park and picnic site, OS 153: TL 073394). Forestry Commission.

Waymarked forest walks of different lengths start from opposite the picnic site. This large wood includes conifer plantations on the greensand at the south end, mixed woodland on the clay at the north end and some attractive flowery meadows in the middle. Wide rides and several small ponds add variety. A special study by the Bedfordshire Natural History Society has shown it to have a very rich flora, with some species, such as the wild service-tree, which indicate that parts have been wooded continuously since the last ice age. Chinese muntjac deer are abundant, and there is a small population of the beautiful but secretive Lady Amherst's pheasant, originally released into the wild from Woburn in about 1900. The best time to visit is between April and October.

Old Warden Tunnel, Old Warden (site entrance, OS 153: TL 114446). Park on the verge of the Old Warden to Cardington road at TL 112444. The reserve can be reached by taking the bridleway (the Greensand Ridge Walk) north-east towards Sweetbriar Farm. Leased by the Wildlife Trust.

The railway running south from Bedford to Hitchin was closed in 1963 after 106 years of use. This attractive nature reserve consists of a deep steep-sided railway cutting and a tunnel top giving fine views to the north. The tunnel top is now covered with hawthorn, attracting flocks of fieldfares in the autumn. The cutting used to be scythed twice a year to prevent spark fires from trains. Flowery grassland is still its main feature, with plants such as cowslips, hairy violets and oxeye daisies, and an abundance of butterflies. Do not enter the tunnel, which is not part of the reserve.

Pegsdon Hills, Pegsdon (entrance, OS 166: TL 118301). Park in Pegsdon village, not on the B655 Barton to Hitchin road). The Wildlife Trust.

This lovely area of Chiltern chalk downland was purchased by the Trust in 1992. Steep dry valleys give incredible views looking north from their upper slopes. Scrub, mostly of hawthorn and often draped in traveller's joy, covers part of the reserve, but there are large areas of grazed grassland with typical chalk flowers such as common rock-rose, salad burnet and devil's-bit scabious. A 10 acre (4 hectare) wood named Hoo Bit at the south end of the reserve lies in Hertfordshire. A prominent wood bank with ancient coppiced beech trees marks the county boundary. There are waymarked circular walks starting from the B655 and the Icknield Way (see page 54) skirts the reserve's southern edge. About half the area used to be arable. The Trust is in the process of returning this to grassland while keeping a small area cultivated as a haven for arable 'weeds', many of which are now becoming rare. Pegsdon Hills are always worth visiting, throughout the year.

Potton Woods, Potton (water tower, OS 153: TL 247495). Forestry Commission.

This large hilltop wood lies on the ill-drained boulder clay. Much has been replanted with conifers, but the east end is still a typical oak, ash, maple and hazel-coppiced woodland with wood anemones, bluebells, early purple orchids, bugle, primroses and oxlips. The last are at their most westerly site in Britain. Woodcock and nightingales breed in the wood, and Chinese muntjac deer can be heard barking. The best time to visit is from April to September and wellington boots should be worn.

Priory Country Park, Bedford (car parks, OS 153: TL 072495 and TL 080489). North Bedfordshire Borough Council.

The country park contains a variety of habitats, including a large gravel pit, flooded in the late 1970s, a smaller area of older gravel workings called the Finger Lakes, parts of the former fishponds of Newnham Priory, a stretch of the river Great Ouse with an old millpool, and many acres of newly planted trees, bushes and grassland. The pits have nesting mallard and grebes and in winter form a refuge for a variety of wildfowl. Larks sing over the grassland and herons fish from the man-made island in the large pit. On the north bank of this pit is an interpretative centre, where the Wildlife Trust has its Bedford headquarters (telephone: 01234 364213). Nature-trail guides and programmes of guided walks are obtainable from the centre. The country park is interesting all the year round.

Putnoe Wood, Bedford (entrance at southwest corner, OS 153: TL 065525). North Bedfordshire Borough Council. Information boards at the main entrances. The two car parks of Mowsbury Park give convenient access to the west edge of the wood. One is off Wentworth Drive, almost opposite Brecon Way (TL 063523) and the other off Kimbolton Road (B660) just north of the town boundary sign (TL 061528). Local Nature Reserve.

The attractive rectangular wood lies on heavy boulder clay on the northern edge of Bedford, surrounded by parkland, playing fields and a golf course. There is a network of firm well-defined paths, much used by dog walkers. The tree cover is mostly of oaks of various ages, with a few ash and an occasional Scots pine and crab apple. Some of the trees are festooned with ivy, which covers the woodland floor in places. The understorey is of hazel and hawthorn, coppiced in the northern, wetter half of the wood. In spring there is a good display of primroses, wood anemones and bluebells. The wood is pleasant to visit at all times of year.

Rowney Warren, near Shefford (car park, OS 153: TL 124404). Forestry Commission.

A waymarked trail starts from the car park. Rowney Warren was formerly a heather-covered heath on the greensand. It is now planted with a variety of conifers, but oak, birch and sweet chestnut are still present, and the wider rides still retain some heather as well as other greensand plants such as heath bedstraw and lesser stitchwort. Bluebells, wood sage, foxgloves and red campion can be found in shadier places. Goldcrests and tits feed in the conifers. Rowney Warren is attractive all the year round.

Sewell Cutting, Houghton Regis (OS 165 and 166: TL 004227 to SP 995227, French's Avenue, Dunstable, to Sewell). Managed by the Wildlife Trust for South Bedfordshire District Council.

The Dunstable to Leighton Buzzard railway, closed in 1962, passed here through a deep chalk cutting. Unlike other Bedfordshire cuttings, which run north-south, Sewell Cutting runs east-west with a sunny south-

The Sundon Hills Country Park, with Sharpenhoe Clappers in the distance.

facing slope and a shady northern slope. The cutting is rich in chalk flowers such as cowslips, oxeye daisies, greater knapweed and field scabious and its sheltered nature makes it excellent for butterflies. The best time to visit is June to September.

In 1859, while the railway cutting was under construction, a shaft 1 metre (3 feet 3 inches) in diameter and 33 metres (108 feet) deep was found. It was packed with Romano-British pottery, human and animal bones and burnt wood. It was probably a Celtic ritual shaft – an entrance to the underworld. The iron age fort of Maiden Bower (page 61) is immediately above the cutting.

Sharpenhoe Clappers, Sharpenhoe (car park, OS 166: TL 065296). National Trust.

The Clappers are a spur of chalk downs crowned by a grove of beech trees, planted in the mid nineteenth century, affording marvellous views to the north. Sycamores are invading the beech, and hawthorn and elder scrub have colonised part of the chalk slopes. Elsewhere the downland is colourful in summer with rock-roses, horseshoe vetch, milkwort, fairy flax, restharrow and dwarf thistle. Slopes

that have recently been cleared of scrub are colonised by wild mignonette, greater knapweed and bladder campion. Under the beeches sanicle forms drifts, while ploughman's spikenard is a feature of the banks beside the path. The Clappers are interesting to visit all the year.

Stewartby Lake Country Park, Marston Moretaine (car park, OS 153: TL 006430). Bedfordshire County Council.

The park covers 318 acres (128 hectares), of which 287 acres (116 hectares) are a huge square water-filled clay pit. In spite of intensive use for water sports, the pit holds the largest winter roost for gulls in the region and attracts many other species of water birds and waders. Excavation of brick clay ceased in 1951, but there has been considerable earth moving and dumping in more recent times, especially on the south side of the pit. The clay banks therefore show different stages of plant colonisation. The older areas are colourful in summer with spiny restharrow, agrimony, wild carrot, wild parsnip and melilot, while colt's-foot, rosebay willowherb and common centaury are a feature of more recently disturbed areas. There are a number of attractive inlets, ditches and shallow pools which are excellent for dragonflies and provide feeding grounds for snipe, redshank and kingfishers. The area is attractive all the year round, but especially good for birds in autumn and winter.

Stockgrove Country Park, Heath and Reach (car park, OS 165: SP 920294). Telephone: 01525 237760. Bedfordshire and Buckinghamshire County Councils. Visitor centre, leaflets, picnic facilities and toilets.

Originally part of two adjoining eighteenth-century estates, its most recent owner was Sir Michael Kroyer Kielberg, who died in 1958. During the Second World War it was used for military training. It is the park to the east which forms the Country Park. Lying on acid soil, it consists of 74 acres (30 hectares) of grassy heaths, oak woodlands, conifer plantations, a lake and a series of small marshes. The heath has a good range of plants that flourish on sandy acid soils, including harebells, heather, tormentil and lady's bedstraw. Wet flushes arise where the heath meets the wood and at the edge of the lake, with some unusual plants, including fragrant agrimony and yellow loosestrife. A wide selection of birds can be seen, with goldcrests in the conifers, yellowhammers characteristic of the heath and nuthatches, jays, treecreepers and woodpeckers present in the oak wood. The best time to visit is April to October.

Sundon Hills Country Park, Upper Sundon (car park, OS 166: TL 048285). Bedfordshire County Council.

This is a 93 acre (38 hectare) site along the steep north-facing slope of the chalk downs, with waymarked walks of varying difficulty. There are extensive views to the north stretching from Toddington to Shefford and dominated by Sharpenhoe Clappers. Most of the hillside is covered with ash woodland with stands of beech and sycamore and pockets of dense scrub of hawthorn, elder, hazel and wayfaring-tree, often shrouded in traveller's joy and black bryony. Patches of original downland with large anthills remain, and there is an old chalk quarry. Both downland and quarry have a characteristic chalk flora with milkwort, woolly thistle, restharrow, rockrose, fairy flax, salad burnet, dwarf thistle, wild basil, common spotted orchids, kidney vetch and ploughman's spikenard. The beech woods have sanicle underneath. Willow warblers and yellowhammers sing in the scrub. The best time to visit is May to October.

Totternhoe Knolls, Totternhoe (car park and picnic site, OS 165: SP 986216). Managed by the Wildlife Trust and Bedfordshire County Council.

A chalk hill topped by a Norman castle mound (see page 62), Totternhoe Knolls commands tremendous views. Old stone quarries called the 'Little Hills' lie at the west end of the site, with a good range of chalk flowers characteristic of disturbed ground, including sainfoin, thyme, kidney vetch and horseshoe vetch. Formerly grazed by sheep and rabbits, the Knolls were invaded by hawthorn scrub when grazing ceased, but much is now being cleared. On the scarp overlooking the village is a mature beech plantation. The best time to visit is June to October.

4
Places of archaeological interest

Some of the earliest discoveries of stone tools of the palaeolithic period were found in the county in the nineteenth century at Biddenham, Caddington, Kempston and Whipsnade. Examples of these can be seen in the Bedford and Luton museums and at the British Museum in London. Although not rich in visible archaeological sites, Bedfordshire has its fair share. Because it is an agricultural county many have been destroyed by ploughing, though they can still be detected on aerial photographs, particularly on the gravels of the Great Ouse and Ivel valleys. The earliest visible sites are on the chalk of the Chilterns in the south. Here the Icknield Way, itself dating from at least 3000 BC, runs east–west across the county and is well worth walking between Pegsdon and north Luton (see Icknield Way Path, page 54). Neolithic burial mounds exist at Pegsdon and Streatley, and another was destroyed in Mill Street, Dunstable.

The county has no visible Roman remains, although it is crossed by two major Roman roads, the Watling Street and Great North Road. Dunstable was the posting station of *Durocobrivis*, and there was a small town at Sandy. Other settlements existed at Luton, Flitwick and near Willington. There is substantial evidence for perhaps two dozen Roman buildings, of which a few may be villas. Examples at Totternhoe, Kempston, Bletsoe and Newnham (Bedford) have been substantiated by excavation.

Bedford Castle, Castle Close, Bedford (OS 153: TL 053496).

The earliest castle was built by Ralf de Tallebosc soon after the Norman conquest. This simple motte and bailey was probably enlarged by Hugh de Beauchamp in the late eleventh century. By 1130 it is recorded that there was 'a strong and unshakable keep'. There was a siege in 1137 and another in 1215. In 1224 Henry III ordered William de Breauté to surrender the castle and when he refused it was besieged for two months, at the end of which the defenders were hanged and the castle was dismantled. The keep was flattened and the ditch filled in. The surviving buildings provided a quarry for Bedford builders for centuries. Today only the motte is clearly visible.

Cainhoe Castle, Clophill (OS 153: TL 098374).

The Norman knight Nigel d'Albini forti-

fied the sandy hilltop. Whether the earthworks we see today were all his work is as yet unknown. Here stands a large high motte, with its original bailey to the west, dug into by an ancient quarry. Around this two later baileys have been built, both well fortified and edged with earthen ramparts that would have taken timber stockades. The ground to the north of the motte falls away steeply to marshy land. A deserted medieval village lies immediately north-west. In the Black Death of 1348-9 the lord of the manor, Peter de St Croix, died, followed by his son Robert and all the villagers. Surely this is why the village was deserted in favour of a new site at Clophill.

Church Spanel, Shillington (OS 153: TL 118350).

This semicircular earthwork consists of a raised platform some 90 metres (295 feet) in diameter with an external bank and ditch on

The motte of Cainhoe Castle, Clophill.

three sides. It is backed by a once navigable stream on the south-east. The whole site is raised some 3 metres (10 feet) above the surrounding marshy land. There are reasons for believing the site may be Danish, but it is open to question.

Conger Hill, Toddington (OS 166: TL 011289).

This well-preserved flat-topped castle motte probably supported a wooden hall during King Stephen's reign. Any surrounding earthworks have been destroyed. This is the scene of the Shrove Tuesday ceremony (see page 108). The name Conger derives from the Old English *conynger*, a rabbit warren.

Five Knolls, Dunstable (OS 166: TL 006210).

This is the finest group of bronze age burial mounds in the Chilterns, consisting of two bowl barrows, three bell barrows and two pond barrows. The most northerly bowl barrow was excavated by Mortimer Wheeler and Gerald Dunning in 1928-9. At the centre was a crouched female burial of late neolithic date. A secondary cremation had been added later. During the Saxon period about thirty bodies were buried in rows with their hands tied behind their backs, the victims of some kind of massacre. Yet more bodies were added to the mound some centuries later, perhaps gallows victims. The finds are in Luton Museum.

The three bell barrows (within a single ditch) have been dug into in the past with no known result. There is no information about the two pond barrows to the east either. They are all of bronze age date.

Galley Hill, Streatley (OS 166: TL 092270).

A round barrow on the summit of Galley Hill covered the remains of fourteen burials of the fourth century AD. They consisted of men and women who may have been slaughtered. Also in the barrow were a neolithic burial and some fifteenth-century gallows victims, together with a witchcraft deposit. There is a second barrow a short distance to the south.

The Hills, Meppershall (OS 153: TL 133358). This is a small well-preserved motte and bailey site on flat land. The motte is 9 metres (30 feet) in diameter, and its rounded top could have taken only a small wooden tower. To the east is an inner bailey about 2.5 metres (8 feet) above the height of the surrounding fields. East again is an outer bailey. There is no clear sign of access from one to the other. The ditches all appear to have been water-filled. The Hills seem to have been the castle of a minor Norman lord, William de Meppershall, and were besieged by King Stephen in 1138.

Howbury, Renhold (OS 153: TL 107513). This perfectly circular earthwork is 40 metres (130 feet) in diameter with a high internal bank and outer ditch. It probably had only one original entrance. It has variously been described as a Roman amphitheatre, a Danish camp and an Anglo-Saxon ringwork. Whilst the writer favours the Danish identification this is by no means certain.

Maiden Bower, Sewell (OS 165: SP 997224). Traces of a neolithic causewayed enclosure were found in the nineteenth century when a row of disconnected pits filled with split ani-

Excavation of one of the Five Knolls at Dunstable by Mortimer Wheeler in 1929.

mal and human bones was destroyed in chalk quarrying. It is possible to see the flat-bottomed neolithic ditches in the edge of the adjoining quarry.

In the iron age a plateau fort was constructed over the top of the disused causewayed site. It enclosed 4.5 hectares (6 acres). Early twentieth-century excavation of the south-east entrance suggests that it was funnel-shaped with a bridge over the top. There is some evidence to indicate that around 350 BC the fort was subjected to fighting with slingstones and resultant slaughter.

Sharpenhoe Clappers, Sharpenhoe (OS 166: TL 066302). National Trust.

This hill spur was fortified during the iron age with a wooden stockade and ditch, which cut it off from the main hill mass and which ran along the edge of the modern beech wood. In the medieval period a mound of earth was piled up, which seems to have been used as an artificial rabbit warren.

Totternhoe Castle and quarries, Totternhoe (OS 165: SP 978221).

This was Bedfordshire's strongest motte and bailey, dramatically sited on a spur of the Chilterns overlooking the Ouzel valley. The name Totternhoe means 'hill spur near the look-out house' and is of Saxon origin, so a look-out house was in existence before the Norman castle was constructed. When, or by whom, this was done is not known, but we can still see a substantial motte with a bailey to the north-west. It is probable that a small wooden tower stood on top of the mound. Later, a second larger bailey was added round the eastern side of the motte, possibly linked to the first by a small timber bridge. This eastern bailey contains the curious 'Money Pit', which was probably a well and was once roofed over. A third, so-called outer, bailey lies to the south-east and may have enclosed a small settlement. In 1169 the castle was known as Eglemunt (Eagle's Hill).

To the north-east of the castle lie the extensive modern chalk quarries. These were first worked in the twelfth century to reveal the

layer of rock in the Lower Chalk known as Totternhoe stone, and frequently referred to in this guide. The stone was 7 metres (23 feet) thick at Totternhoe and was in much demand for royal buildings, abbeys and churches during the middle ages. By the nineteenth century hundreds of passages honeycombed the hills, and people were easily lost in them. The last tunnel was officially sealed about 1914, but modern quarry equipment occasionally breaks through into one of them.

Waulud's Bank, Leagrave (OS 166: TL 062247).

It is still possible to detect a semicircular bank 2.5 metres (8 feet) high in places, and a ditch 6 metres (20 feet) wide, sweeping from the source of the Lea in the Sundon Road recreation ground towards Bramingham Road. Excavations in 1953 and 1971 suggest that the site is of two periods: at first a domestic habitation and then a henge monument used by people who hunted and fished, as well as reared cattle, beside the Lea marshes. Situated close to the spot where the Icknield Way fords the river Lea, it would have been well positioned as a ceremonial meeting place. Occupation was probably between 3000 and 2500 BC.

Yielden Castle, Yelden (OS 153: TL 013670).

These well-preserved earthworks consist of a large motte 27 metres (90 feet) by 40 metres (130 feet) and 12 metres (40 feet) high. On its south-west is an inner bailey, with another to the north. There seems to have been a long narrow fishpond on the western side and a series of small enclosures on the east. Slight excavation in 1881 showed that there had been a stone wall around the inner bailey and that a small island in the fishpond had provided a base for a round tower 9 metres (30 feet) in diameter. Foundations on top of the motte had been robbed, perhaps to build the church. The castle was built by the Norman Trailly family, but we know little of them. By 1361 the castle was in ruins and the family extinct.

5
Churches

This chapter contains only churches considered to be of outstanding interest. Other references will be found in chapter 2. Most churches are kept locked, but some have notices of keyholders in the porch.

Ampthill: St Andrew.
This ironstone church was first built in the mid twelfth century, but largely rebuilt in the fifteenth. The roof has been restored, though most of the angels are partly fifteenth-century. In the chancel stands a genuine Roman column set up to commemorate the Earl of Upper Ossory (died 1828). North of the altar is the tomb of Colonel Richard Nicolls, who died at the battle of Sole Bay off Southwold, Suffolk, in 1672. The cannonball which killed him is set in the pediment above the monument. Two modern windows are of interest in the north aisle: one recalls the Ampthill National School, 1845-1954, and the other shows Sir John Cornwall, who built Ampthill Castle, with his wife Princess Elizabeth. Unveiled in 1982, it is based on an engraving of an earlier window long since lost. Behind the church is a fine modern octagonal chapter-house.

Aspley Guise: St Botolph. (South-east of Milton Keynes, between M1 and A513.)
The church was heavily restored in 1855. The tower, north aisle and part of the nave contain original fourteenth-century work; the font might be earlier. There is a tomb-chest in the north chapel looking oddly out of place. On it lies a war-worn knight in armour, possibly Sir William Tyryngton. Under the floor carpet are brasses to a knight (c.1500) and a priest with St John the Baptist (c.1410).

Astwick: St Guthlac. (South of Biggleswade, east of A1.)
St Guthlac was a seventh-century 'young blood' from Lincolnshire, who was converted to the spiritual life and lived out his days as a hermit in the fens at Crowland. The building is of ironstone pebbles and Totternhoe stone and appears to have once had a south transept, on the evidence of a tall blocked arch in the south face of the tower. There are early graffiti on the east end of the church. Inside are eighteenth-century box pews and a two-decker pulpit.

Barton in the Clay: St Nicholas. (North of Luton, bypassed by A6.)
Most of the church building is thirteenth-century in date, though the tower belongs to the mid fifteenth century. The clerestory and nave roof are slightly later, having carved angels, apostles and bosses. There appears to have been a living room on the first floor of the tower. Strangely it has a fireplace with no chimney and a door which opens into space. There are brasses to Philip de Lee (died 1340) and Richard Brey (died 1396).

Battlesden: St Peter. (North-east of Leighton Buzzard, off A4012.)
The church has been patched many times with sandstone, Totternhoe stone and red and yellow brick. A fifteenth-century tower has been built into a thirteenth-century nave. The chancel was probably built in the early fourteenth century, though only the chancel arch remains to confirm it. The font is Norman and drum-shaped with simple carvings, including lilies. Stains on the red-glazed tiles show that rain often flows in from the north porch, which is on a higher level than the nave. There are wall monuments to the Duncombe family, who held the manor in the seventeenth century, and on either side of the Victorian east windows are recut angels of about 1500.

Bedford: St Mary.
The church is now in the care of the Bedfordshire County Council and is known as St Mary's Church Archaeology Centre (see page 93). Part of the tower and south transept seems

to date from the eleventh century, whilst the nave was rebuilt in the twelfth century and the chancel in the fourteenth and nineteenth centuries. The north aisle is sixteenth-century and the south Victorian. There are three medieval coffin lids near the altar. The bowl of the font came from the demolished church of St Peter de Dunstable, which once stood opposite, on what is now St Mary's Square.

Bedford: St Paul.

The exterior is mainly fourteenth- and fifteenth-century, though the tower and spire are modern. The nave is almost entirely a late nineteenth-century rebuild, except for the arches of the south arcade, which are mostly early fourteenth-century. The wide high aisles create a spacious hall effect. The roof, supported by carved figures and birds, is fifteenth-century, as is the parclose screen at the entrance to the Trinity Chapel. There are misericords in the choir, including one depicting an archer driving Falkes de Breauté from the castle. John Wesley is reputed to have preached from a pulpit in the nave. In the south chapel are brasses to Sir William Harpur and his second wife, whilst in front of the altar in the sanctuary is the burial slab of Simon de Beauchamp (died 1208).

Bedford: St Peter de Merton.

This is an aisleless Anglo-Saxon church with tower which was heavily restored and enlarged by the Victorians. The present chancel was the Anglo-Saxon nave, and the choir and organ under the tower can be considered as the site of the original entrance or narthex; the present chancel arch is nineteenth-century. Traces of long and short quoins can be found inside and outside. The south doorway is Norman but brought from the demolished church of St Peter de Dunstable.

Biddenham: St James. (Just west of Bedford, south of A428.)

There is a Norman arch and windows though most periods of architecture are represented in this interesting building. The screen to the Lady Chapel is sixteenth-century. There is a fine monument to Sir William Boteler (died 1601) and his wife, Ursula. Their fam-

ily lived in the village for four centuries. Displayed in the tower is a clarinet played in the church orchestra by James West almost until his death in 1861.

Biggleswade: St Andrew.

The exterior of the church dates mostly from the restoration of 1884, with further changes after the fire of 1953 and the addition of a chapter-house in 1976. The grey stone tower was rebuilt in 1720. Most of the internal changes were made by John Ruding about 1470, when he built the chancel and raised the nave roof. He also prepared his tomb in the chancel, which still has parts of his brass remaining, but he was buried in Buckinghamshire, not Biggleswade. Also in the chancel are three fine sedilia and a piscina. Above the fifteenth-century porch is a room that was once used as a school. There is a tombstone to Mary Tealby (died 1865), a founder of the Battersea Dogs Home, on the north-west of the churchyard.

Bletsoe: St Mary. (North of Bedford, just east of A6.)

This is a large limestone church with a thirteenth-century nave and fourteenth-century central tower, chancel and south transept. The north transept is Victorian, and the whole building was heavily restored in 1858 and later. We are told that the windows are exact copies of the originals. The chancel is now closed off from the rest of the building and not in use. In the north transept is a fine alabaster monument to Sir John St John (died 1559) and his wife, with their nine children behind them. Another monument recalls Frances, Countess Bolingbroke (died 1678). There is also a modern stained glass window in the nave illustrating the four hundredth anniversary of the printing of the Bible.

Blunham: St James or St Edmund. (Northwest of Sandy, west of A1.)

The church is light and airy with tall thin pillars of the early fifteenth century. The lower part of the tower is Norman, with a large arch into the nave and the west doorway both decorated with alternate limestone and ironstone voussoirs. The chancel is thirteenth-century. In the north wall is a recessed tomb or Easter sepulchre of about 1350 with elaborate heavy foliar decoration around it. Opposite is a tomb with a recumbent alabaster figure of Susan Longueville, Countess of Kent (died 1620). There is a fine stone screen of late fifteenth-century date between the chancel and the Lady Chapel. In the latter is a case containing fragments of alabaster carved in the fourteenth and fifteenth centuries. A monument to Godfrey Thornton (died 1805), a director of the Bank of England, is decorated with a sailing ship and an ox, tropical fruit and corn. John Donne was incumbent here in the seventeenth century, but there is little evidence that he ever spent much time living in the village.

Bolnhurst: St Dunstan. (North of Bedford, on B660.)

Standing amongst trees, St Dunstan's is mainly Perpendicular in style, perhaps fifteenth-century. The screen has been much restored, the pulpit is Jacobean, and the organ case designed by A. W. N. Pugin. There is a

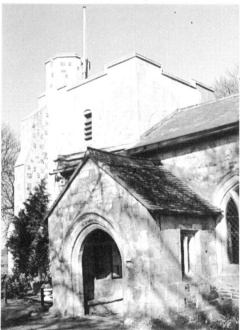

Chalgrave church.

sadly faded wall painting of St Christopher above the north door. A marble monument of John Francklin (died 1707) is of note. He was the last of the family at Bolnhurst. Outside the south door is the worn stump of a cross.

Bromham: St Owen. (West of Bedford, by-passed by A428.)

The church was restored by Butterfield in 1868, though the nave is still mostly thirteenth-century and the tower fifteenth-century. The room above the porch once held a library given by Lord Trevor in 1740. A brass commemorating Thomas Wydvile (died 1435) and his two wives was appropriated by Sir John Dyve (died 1535) and a strip of brass was inserted claiming the figures as his wife and mother. There is a fine recumbent monument of Sir Lewis Dyve (died 1603) and a touching Gothic memorial to twelve-year-old Eva Trevor (died 1842), shown floating heavenwards.

Campton: All Saints. (South-west of Shefford, off A507.)

In the graveyard is the tombstone of Robert Bloomfield (see Shefford, page 32, and page 101), a minor poet, whose most famous work, *The Farmer's Boy*, sold 26,000 copies in less than three years. The church dates mostly from about 1300 with some restoration of 1900. On the north side is a seventeenth-century chapel for the Osborne family of Chicksands Priory, which contains two large marble altar tombs for Sir Peter and Sir John Osborne erected in 1655.

Chalgrave: All Saints. (South of Toddington, by A5120. OS 166: TL 008275.)

The deserted medieval manor of Chalgrave lay to the south-east of the church. Aerial photographs have recorded it, but it was sadly bulldozed and ploughed in the 1960s. The thirteenth-century church stands isolated but well cared for, and it is of great importance since it contains a magnificent collection of wall paintings, now somewhat faded, but being restored. The pictures range in date from the late thirteenth century to the fifteenth, with some eighteenth-century texts. The earliest work is to be seen at the west end of both aisles, where the Twelve Apostles are shown beneath trefoiled canopies. Above the arches of the nave and continuing into the aisles are the remains of eighteen shields of arms, flanked by a foliage border. The shields celebrate the Loring family and its connections and date from about 1370. Over the south door is St Martin of Tours, painted about 1400, with St Christopher on the north wall facing visitors as they enter. There are two good table tombs, sadly defaced by modern graffiti. They are probably those of Sir Nigel (or Nele) Loring (died 1386) and another member of his family. In the churchyard is the grave of Enoch Bennett, father of the novelist Arnold Bennett. Arnold lived at Trinity Hall Farm near the Watling Street for three years (1900-3). His detective novel *Teresa of Watling Street* is set at the farm and the neighbouring village of Hockliffe.

Clapham: St Thomas of Canterbury. (Northwest of Bedford, on A6.)

The tower, 26 metres (85 feet) high, is one of the wonders of Bedfordshire. The lower 18 metres (59 feet) are pure Saxon, except for the west door, which is a later addition. The top 8 metres (26 feet) are Norman. It has been suggested that the tower was originally built for defence against the Danes. It is not impossible but cannot be substantiated. The nave arches are thirteenth-century, but the rest of the church is a rebuilding by George Gilbert Scott in 1861.

Clifton: All Saints. (East of Shefford, north of A507.)

The church has a pleasant little nave and chancel of about 1320, to which has been added a fifteenth-century Perpendicular tower. The north aisle and chapel were rebuilt by Edward Haycock in 1862. In the nave is a blocked fifteenth-century window which gave light to an altar. The font, carved from Purbeck marble, of thirteenth-century date, is the oldest surviving feature. Hidden in the north chapel is a splendid alabaster table tomb, made for Sir Thomas Lucy (died 1525) and

his wife, whose beautifully carved effigies lie upon it. It is not known why it was moved to Clifton from Grey Friars in London soon after it was made. Sir Thomas's bare head rests upon a helm with lion's crest, he wears plate armour and carries a sword and dagger. His hands are broken. Lady Lucy has a jewelled chaplet in her hair, and her cloak is fastened with a skilfully carved cord across her chest. Two angels, once at her head, have been vandalised in the twentieth century. But vandalism is nothing new. Both figures are covered with graffiti, some of them more than two hundred years old, and now interesting in their own right. An ancient rood screen, now at the entrance to the choir vestry, has late fourteenth-century paintings upon it, which are currently undergoing restoration.

Cockayne Hatley: St John the Baptist. (East of Potton, north of B1042.)

The tiny village lies amongst the prairies, close to the Cambridgeshire border. The tall Perpendicular tower of the church is crowned by four pinnacles. The body of the church dates from the thirteenth century, but at Cockayne Hatley it is not the fabric but the furnishings which engage our eyes. In the early nineteenth century the Honourable and Reverend Henry Cockayne Cust found the church in a most lamentable state of neglect and undertook a major restoration, completed by 1830. As well as much rebuilding, he installed in the church a unique treasury of baroque woodwork from Belgium. The tower screen is from Louvain, the communion rail from Malines. The stalls and stall backs with rich Catholic carving are from Aulne Abbey near Charleroi (dated 1689), and there is much more. There is some good stained glass of fourteenth- and fifteenth-century date which originated in Yorkshire. In the floor of the nave are some of the finest brasses in the county, representing the Cockayne families of the fifteenth and sixteenth centuries.

The churchyard contains the tomb of W. E. Henley, the nineteenth-century poet and writer (1849-1903). As a boy he lost the lower part of a leg. He was a friend of R. L. Stevenson and became the model for Long John Silver. He also had a friendship with

Part of the monument to Sir William Dyer and his family in Colmworth church.

J. M. Barrie, and his daughter Margaret is said to have inspired the character of Wendy in *Peter Pan*. She died aged five and is buried beside her father.

Colmworth: St Denys. (North-east of Bedford, east of B660.)

The tall oaks and old tiled barn along the church drive invite one to visit this beautiful Perpendicular building, probably created for Sir Gerard Braybrook within the span of four years between 1426 and 1430 by an architect of distinction. It is dedicated to the French saint in honour of Sir Gerard's French wife, Eleanor. The treasure of the church is the alabaster monument to Sir William Dyer, erected by his wife in 1641. Part of the inscription, perhaps written by Lady Catherine, reads: 'Mine eyes wax heavy, and the days grow old, The dew falls thick, my blood grows cold. Draw, draw the loosed curtains and make the room, My dear, my dearest dust, I come, I come.'

Restoration work has been completed in the tower and the six bells have been rehung.

On the north side of the churchyard is the chest-tomb of Timothy Matthews, an evangelist, who was curate at Colmworth for twelve years until he became a Wesleyan and moved to Bedford. He is remembered for striding round the county town calling folk to worship by blowing a copper trumpet. He died of typhus in 1845 and was buried in Bedford, being moved to Colmworth soon afterwards.

Cople: All Saints. (East of Bedford, south of A603.)

Cople is a rather unexciting village, but All Saints' church is splendid. Built in the fifteenth century, it contains a rich collection of brasses gathered at the eastern end, ranging from Nicholas Roland of about 1400 to Robert Bulkeley (died 1550) and his wife Joan (died 1556). It is perhaps surprising that any remain today; John Byng wrote in 1794: 'returning to Cople Church we stopped for the inspection; in which are some old Luke tombs; and some brasses, but *none* that would travel.'

Dunstable: St Peter.

The church is all that remains of Henry I's priory, the rest having been demolished after the Dissolution. The magnificent Norman nave, unfortunately lacking its clerestory, and thus its original height, and the great west door arch survive. The two west towers fell in 1222, and only the north was rebuilt. On either side of the high altar are the outlines of doors which led into the canons' choir. The church's treasured embroidery, the Fayrey Pall, is now in the Victoria and Albert Museum in London.

Eaton Bray: St Mary. (West of Dunstable, east of A4146.)

St Mary's church was built in the thirteenth century with Tottemhoe stone and consider-

The mid thirteenth-century ironwork on the door of Eaton Bray church.

ably modified in the fifteenth, when only the Early English arcades survived. Nineteenth-century graffiti in the porch bear comparison with those on the church hall next door. The tower dates from about 1320. The nave is early thirteenth-century, with delightful arcades, each of five bays, decorated with stiff-leaf carvings. The magnificent font echoes these and is of similar date. The south doorway has fine ironwork of the mid thirteenth century, perhaps by Thomas of Leighton. There are two firehooks hanging inside the church. They were used to pull burning thatch or beams from a cottage roof.

Edworth: St George. (South-east of Biggleswade, east of A1.)

The church is reached from the southbound carriageway of the A1 by a narrow metalled track. The nave is probably thirteenth-century, with aisles and chancel added about 1320. Features include a square pillar piscina, a badly faded wall painting and a little fourteenth- and fifteenth- century glass. There are fifteenth-century animal carvings on the chancel seats, and a large iron-bound parish chest with iron wheels.

Elstow: St Mary. (Just south of Bedford, east of A6.)

St Mary's, the original abbey church, contains massive Norman piers and arches, and some of the thirteenth century. The church was most insensitively restored and indeed partially rebuilt by T. G. Jackson in 1881. The north door, for example, once Norman, now has hardly an original stone left, although above it on the outside is a panel of about 1140 showing Christ with St Peter and St John. One survival of the nunnery is a small vaulted room now used as a vestry. The church has a detached bell-tower of fifteenth-century date. John Bunyan was baptised in the church font.

Eversholt: St John. (South-west of Ampthill, and east of Woburn.)

St John's church was built of ironstone in the early fourteenth and fifteenth centuries. The font is thirteenth-century and the piscina about 1330. A feature of the church is the wall paintings (actually on canvas) by Edward Aveling Green (1842-1930), who lived at Berrystead in Eversholt. His pictures are competent and romantic but show a certain sameness, which is not surprising since he used the same local girl as a model for most of them. His statue of St Michael stands on the war memorial in the churchyard.

Everton: St Mary. (North-east of Sandy, north of B1042.)

Everton stands on a hill with the greensand escarpment to the west. The tower of St Mary's church was struck by lightning in 1974 and has been shortened, leaving insufficient room for its five bells, which were sold to a church in Chicago. Apart from the fifteenth-century chancel, the interior is almost entirely late Norman, with splendid arcade arches and south doorway. In the nave the piercing eyes of Sir Humphrey Winche follow the visitor from his monument above the pulpit. As a judge he earned an unhappy reputation after sentencing nine women to death for witchcraft at Leicester Assizes in 1616. In the churchyard is the fascinating tomb of the Reverend John Betridge (1716-93), whose life story it tells.

Felmersham: St Mary. (North-west of Bedford, west of A6.)

St Mary's is the finest Early English church in the county, built between 1220 and 1240 with very little alteration. The arcaded west front is an architectural gem. In the fifteenth century the nave walls were raised, allowing clerestory windows to be inserted. This produced an interior of monumental cathedral proportions, with the massive central tower supported on four great arches and clusters of columns. The delicate fifteenth-century oak screen was erected by Richard and Annette Kyng and is decorated with tiny angels and coloured in faded red, blue and gold. The modern green window glass is a most helpful addition to this magnificent building.

Flitwick: St Peter. (South of Ampthill, on A5120.)

On the north side of the church is a reset Norman doorway with good beakhead orna-ment and stupid modern graffiti. The painted and fluted font is also Norman. The south arcade and doorway date from the thirteenth century, and the tower perhaps two centuries later. There is a Jacobean pulpit and a fine new octagonal chapter-house.

Harlington: St Mary. (South of Ampthill, east of A5120.)

The church is mainly late thirteenth-century, with delicate nave arches. The windows are mostly sixteenth-century, though two blocked earlier examples can still be seen. The fifteenth-century nave roof is original, as are a few of the corbels. Notice one in which a man leads a dragon by a rope round its neck, whilst another dragon attacks him. There are also two wall monuments, one to James Astrey (died 1716) and another to Katherine Arnold (died 1681): 'Short was thy life, Yet livest thou ever, Death hath his due, Yet diest thou never.'

Harrold: St Peter. (North-west of Bedford, north of A428.)

St Peter's church is tall and light. Much of it is thirteenth-century. The late fourteenth-century tower has a fine ancient roof, and the bellringing chamber opens directly into the nave. The rood screen is partly fifteenth-century and partly Jacobean. In the chancel is a large altar tomb with a brown marble top to Oliver Boteler (died 1657) and his son William (died 1703). The family once lived at Harrold Hall (now demolished).

Higham Gobion: St Margaret. (North of Luton, east of A6.)

A well-kept and simple little church of Totternhoe stone and greenstone, St Margaret's was built early in the fourteenth century and heavily restored in 1880. The tower was originally shorter and supported a squat pyramid-shaped belfry. The year of the Armada is recorded on a beam above the chancel arch, together with the initials HB, almost certainly those of Sir Henry Butler, lord of the manor. There are also brasses of the Butler ladies with their children, on the wall beside the sedilia in the chancel. Also in the chancel is a monument to Edmund Castell,

Kensworth church with its Victorian patterned roof.

rector from 1662 to 1685, a Semitic scholar and Professor of Arabic at Cambridge. He wrote a dictionary in seven oriental languages called *Lexicon Heptaglotton.* It was a masterpiece but not recognised as such at the time. Many unsold copies were destroyed in the Great Fire of London or eaten by rats in Higham rectory. In 1684 Castell was in trouble with the Bishop of Lincoln for allowing one of his unordained students to preach three times at Higham 'which hath but five houses'. The Bishop of London pleaded on his behalf and was rewarded with part of Castell's extensive library. He set up his own monument in the church in 1662, twenty-three years before he died. It includes the oldest carved Arabic inscription in England, which reads: 'Living, here he chose to be buried, in hopes of a better place than this.'

Houghton Conquest: All Saints. (South of Bedford, east of B530.)

This is a large and light church. Building began on the tower in 1393 according to a contract which still exists. The masons came from Dunstable and Totternhoe and had three years to complete the work. The rest of the building dates from earlier in the fourteenth century. There are wall paintings, now some-

what faded. Over the chancel arch is a figure of Christ, painted soon after the building was completed. Above the north door stands St Christopher, and in the south aisle are traces of St George and the dragon. The hexagonal font is fourteenth-century. Amusing stall-heads in the chancel include angels, dragons, dogs and deacons. There is a chest-tomb with brasses of Isabel Conquest (died 1493) and her husband and son, the two men identically portrayed. The monument to Dr Thomas Archer, showing him preaching, was erected during his lifetime, in 1629 when he was seventy. In the outside wall of the chancel is a tomb recess for Thomas Awdley (died 1531).

Hulcote: St Nicholas. (East of Milton Keynes, north of A421. OS 153: SP 944389.)

Rooktree Farm and the seventeenth-century Hulcot Manor stand at either end of a splendid avenue of lime trees, which leads past St Nicholas's church, the treasure of the parish. Originally a private chapel, it was rebuilt by Richard Chernocke about 1590. His initials are set in nails on the door. It is a fine example of a small Elizabethan country church. The windows are mullioned and transomed, and only the tower arch is Perpendicular. The white-painted ceiling is tunnel-vaulted. Beside the altar is the repainted monument to Richard Chernocke (died 1615). It shows Richard and his wife with their eight girls and six boys, and his father, Robert, with two wives and ten children. Only the eighteenth-century font looks uncomfortable in this lovely quiet building.

Kempston: All Saints. (South-west of Bedford.)

All Saints' church, commissioned by the Conqueror's niece Judith in 1100, stands beside the Ouse. The arches of the tower and chancel are Norman, the aisles and chancel thirteenth-century. In the fifteenth century the tower and nave walls were heightened, and the south porch with priest's chamber above was added. There is a medieval wall painting on the west wall of the nave.

Kensworth: St Mary. (South of Dunstable, west of A5.)

St Mary's church is a large building with a Perpendicular west tower, built partly in the local tradition of chequered flint and Totternhoe stone. On the north side narrow Norman windows are visible. In the south porch is an attractive Romanesque doorway with interlaced decoration, and one of its capitals illustrating a fox and crane fable. The west door linking the nave and tower, as well as most of the chancel, dates from about 1120. Alterations were made in the fifteenth century when the east window and adjoining niches were added. The usual Victorian restoration took place in 1878.

Keysoe: St Mary. (North of Bedford, on B660.)

Keysoe is one of those parishes that is made up of 'ends'. St Mary's church is a cream limestone building well away from any settlement. It has a splendid fourteenth-century tower capped by a tall spire. The interior is dignified yet simple. There are fascinating 'primitive' corbels in the north aisle, and unusual, well-carved bench ends. A curious feature is an inscription on the font base, written in fourteenth-century French, which is best translated: 'You who pass by, for the soul of Warel pray that God by his grace will be truly merciful.' The church is best-known for the inscription on the outside of the tower which records in great detail how in 1718 William Dickins fell from the spire, crying

The story of William Dickins's miraculous escape, on Keysoe church tower.

Knotting church, with its restored preaching cross.

out to his brother: 'Lord! Daniel! Wots the matter? Lord have mercy upon me!' The Lord did, for he lived for another forty-one years. Opposite the churchyard gate is an interesting brick bier house.

Knotting: St Margaret. (South-east of Rushden, east of A6.)

Farm, church and houses are pleasantly grouped at a bend in the road. St Margaret's church is fascinating. The tiny limestone tower is dated 1615, but the nave is Norman. The chancel arch has fine zigzag ornament, though the tower arch seems to be of local design and undatable. There is a worn tomb slab set into the floor of the chancel. Everywhere there is an air of decay. The Jacobean pulpit with sounding board seems to belong to some Gothic film set. One cannot fail to notice the chancel gates, set up in 1637 after cock fighting had taken place in the chancel on Shrove Tuesday in the presence of the rector and churchwardens. There is a sundial on the south wall of the church, and a churchyard cross with medieval base and well-restored modern top.

Leighton Buzzard: All Saints.

All Saints' church, with its 58 metre (190 foot) spire, draws worshippers from all directions. Begun about 1277, the plan of the church has altered little, although a splendid East Anglian style clerestory was added to the nave about 1470 by the Duchess of Suffolk, and about the same time beautiful angel roofs were hung throughout the building. On 13th April 1985 the church was suddenly devastated by a great fire which swept through the chancel roof and into the tower, raging up the spire like a chimney, and on into the nave roof, on the way destroying totally Bodley's choir organ, chancel windows and some of the recently rehung bells. Most of the damage was confined to the upper parts of the building, and much of the nave roof survived. The transepts were safe and we can still see the original painted angels, some of them in their leathered tights, as they may have appeared in the local mystery plays. The cauldron-like font is older than the present church, as is the sanctus bell, called Ting-Tang. The thirteenth-century oak eagle lectern, possibly the oldest in Britain, also survived the fire. Most intriguing are numerous medieval graffiti on columns in the nave and crossing area. Unfortunately many have been badly obliterated by lime washing. Noteworthy are the drawings of windows, birds, shields and geometric patterns. In the north-west corner of the south transept is a deep relief carving, known as Simon and Nelly, in which a man and woman are seen perhaps making a Sim-Nel cake. The church has a large number of windows designed by C. E. Kempe (1834-1907). The great west door is decorated with elegant scrolled ironwork and hinges designed by Thomas of Leighton about 1288. Unfortunately it looks out of place remounted on a modern door. More of Thomas's ironwork is on the inside of the north door of the chancel. He went on to make the iron grille for Queen Eleanor's tomb in Westminster Abbey.

Lower Gravenhurst: Our Lady. (South-west of Shefford, south of A507. OS 153: TL 111353.)

This fourteenth-century church, now maintained by the Redundant Churches Fund, has a completely unspoiled interior. The chancel is separated from the nave only by a painted fifteenth-century rood screen. There is a wrought-iron hourglass stand attached to it. The roof has moulded king posts, and the pulpit is Jacobean. There is a brass inscription in the chancel to Robert de Bilhemore, 'who made this church anew' in the fourteenth century. A marble altar tomb marks the resting place of Benjamin Piggot (died 1606) and his three wives.

Luton: St Mary.

Hemmed in by the University, St Mary's is a jewel amidst mediocrity. The present building was begun in the thirteenth century, enlarged in the fourteenth century, and achieved its final glory in the fifteenth century, at which time the soaring, tapering canopy over the Wenlock tombs was completed. One of the largest parish churches in England, St Mary's

In Leighton Buzzard church is the carving thought to represent the making of a Simnel cake.

impresses with its massive chequered flint and limestone façade. Its interior is spacious and one is immediately confronted by the octagonal fourteenth-century baptistry, once painted, but now plain white limestone as first made. Beneath it is the marble font of about 1250. The chancel is much restored but contains an Easter sepulchre and four stone sedilia of late fourteenth-century date. Beside them is the tiny sunken chantry chapel of Richard Barnard, vicar from 1477 to 1492, with the rebus of a bear and box of spikenard (an ointment) carved about it. Between the chancel and the Wenlock Chapel is 'a wide and lofty arch, divided into two by a slight pier'. This is the delicate and sumptuous Wenlock screen, built by Sir John Wenlock in 1461. Beneath it are buried William Wenlock (died 1392) and Lady Alice Rotherham (died 1490?). On the wall in the Wenlock Chapel are two sixteenth-century helmets. There is a brass to John Ackworth (died 1513) with his two wives and seventeen members of the Guild of the Holy Trinity, which he helped to found in Luton in 1471. A brass of Hugo atte Spettyl (died 1416) recalls the leper hospital he founded at Spittlesea, which is now under the runway of Luton Airport. The 'exploding' Magnificat Window of 1979 in the south aisle

is by Alan Younger. Flint has been used sympathetically in building the 1968 Church Hall.

Millbrook: St Michael. (West of Ampthill, north of A507.)

The sandstone church was heavily restored by Butterfield in 1857 and 1864. The south aisle is the oldest part. The north aisle was built in the fifteenth century and the image niche in the north-east corner is noteworthy. The reredos is by Sir Albert Richardson, who, with his wife, lies buried in the graveyard. In the south aisle is a monument to Lord and Lady Holland (died 1840, 1845) and their ten-year-old daughter Georgiana Anne Fox (died 1819). In the chancel are the effigies of William and Mary Huett, who died in 1602. In the mid nineteenth century the figures were moved to the vicarage cellars, and from then onwards curious noises were heard in the church. Only when they were buried in the churchyard was peace restored. This coincided with the removal of rotting roof timbers in 1888. In 1919 the figures were dug up and returned to the chancel, and no noises have been heard since!

Milton Bryan: St Peter. (North-east of Leighton Buzzard, off A4012.)

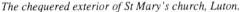

The chequered exterior of St Mary's church, Luton.

St Peter's church is built of every material under the sun. Basically a Norman building, it was drastically restored by Cottingham in 1841-3. The early arches can still be seen, but they have lost their look of antiquity. One column, halfway along the chancel, seems to have escaped restoration. The font is Norman. Near the pulpit is an excellent decorated twelfth-century coffin lid, and there is a marble monument to Sir Hugh Inglis (died 1820) of the East India Company. The church contains two very fine iron-bound chests and a stained glass window commemorating Joseph Paxton, designer of the Crystal Palace, who was born in the parish.

Northill: St Mary. (South-west of Sandy, west of B658.)

St Mary's is a fine sandstone building of the fourteenth century with additions of a century later. It was made collegiate by Henry IV in 1404, and the chancel seems to date from this event. The interior was restored in 1663 and 1862; the nave arcades survive from the fourteenth century, but the chancel arch is a rebuilding of the nineteenth century. Lovers of stained glass should not miss the two glorious windows produced for the Grocers' Company, patrons of the church, by John Oliver in 1664, and richly painted with a bold design incorporating the arms of the company and the escutcheon of Lady Margaret Slaney, who re-endowed the living, and Charles II. The church also contains a parish chest of 1663 and a seventeenth-century bier, bearing the name of Thomas Tompion senior.

Oakley: St Mary. (North-west of Bedford, off A6.)

In a beautiful setting above the river Ouse, there is a remarkable sense of tranquillity around this old church. The tower dates from the middle of the twelfth century and the nave was built not long after, though it is much restored. The chancel dates from about 1220. It was fitted with new pews in the fifteenth century. The finest possessions of the church are the screens in the north and south aisles. That on the north has a loft over it and bears a painting of Christ seated on a rainbow against a background of stars. The southern screen was probably the original rood screen and still shows signs of painting. Outside the south porch is the weathered base of an old preaching cross.

Odell: All Saints. (North-west of Bedford, west of A6.)

Opposite the castle is the fifteenth-century limestone church of All Saints, its lovely chestnut trees in the churchyard brutally truncated. The interior is spacious, with tall arcades. The painted rood screen is fifteenth-century work and there is another screen under the tower arch, the gift of William Alston, who died in 1637. The pulpit and box pews are of the same date. Most of the early window glass has gone but there are some delightful angels in the south aisle.

Old Warden: St Leonard. (West of Biggleswade, west of B658.)

St Leonard's is a church of coursed brown sandstone ashlar cobbles and brickwork. Inside, the tower has a Norman arch, and a few fourteenth-century details occur elsewhere. However, one is overwhelmed by a mass of dark Belgian woodwork, collected by Lord Ongley from 1841 onwards.

Pavenham: St Peter. (North-west of Bedford, west of A6.)

There are heads everywhere in this splendid church, carved on door arches and windows, inside and out, a gallery of the village folk of five hundred years ago. In the north aisle is the finest green man corbel in the county. Uneven floors, sumptuous carved sedilia and an overwhelming mass of Jacobean wood-carving (mainly old bed headboards) brought to the church by the timber-merchant squire Thomas Abbott Green in 1848 help to make this well-loved church amongst the most interesting in Bedfordshire. A Hay Ceremony is held each July (see page 106).

Pertenhall: St Peter. (North of Bedford on B660.)

St Peter's church is largely Perpendicular with a broach spire of Northampton type. There is late Norman work inside, including a

Elaborately decorated niches in Pavenham church.

Potsgrove: St Mary. (North-east of Leighton Buzzard, between A5 and A4012.)

Lanes from north and south meet at this minute village centred on St Mary's church, with the former rectory, Manor Farm and the old school of 1897. Opposite the church is a large moat, part of it still containing water. The churchyard, overgrown with blue comfrey, has some excellent eighteenth- and nineteenth-century gravestones. Plans to demolish St Mary's in 1968 were thwarted by a delegation which included Sir John Betjeman. The Poet Laureate considered it 'most attractively restored' with 'a really delightful interior'. Basically of fourteenth-century date, it was carefully restored in 1881. The rood screen is good fourteenth-century work, with Victorian additions. In the chancel is a medieval tomb recess, with two curious wooden cupboards or aumbries let into it. Beside the altar are brasses to the sixteenth-century Saunders family.

Potton: St Mary. (North-east of Biggleswade on B1040.)

St Mary's church stands proud on a small hill, surrounded by rank upon rank of delightful gravestones dating back to 1690, carved with skulls and angels, and numerous fascinating scripts. Inside, the church is an anticlimax. The fourteenth-century nave is light and airy, the north transept was built a century earlier, whilst the tower and north porch were added in the fifteenth century. A small door leads to a priest's room above the porch.

little dog-tooth ornament. In the north aisle are traces of a wall painting of a seated figure accompanied by saints and an angel. Monuments include a damaged cross-legged knight and tablets to Mary Rolt, daughter of Oliver Cromwell, and Thomas Martyn, Professor of Botany at Cambridge. 'The old weather-worn tombstones that lurched in the tousled churchyard grass' for Bernard West in 1947 have been moved so that the grass may be clinically mown.

Podington: St Mary. (South of Rushden, west of A6.)

Although most of St Mary's is thirteenth-century, part of the chancel is Norman, and it is possible to make out a window in the outside wall. There is also a Norman font, and numerous monuments to the Orlebar family of Hinwick House. The nineteenth-century organ has been restored for the 92nd Bombardment Group of the USAAF as a memorial to their members who died in the Second World War whilst serving at Podington Airfield.

Riseley: All Saints. (North of Bedford, east of A6.)

All Saints' is a pleasant family church with a complicated history. A twelfth-century nave and chancel stood on the site of the present nave. To this the existing south aisle and chapel were added about 1200, in the process altering or removing much of the earlier building. The chancel was enlarged to its present size in the fourteenth century and the tower added about 1400. In the mid nineteenth century, when the arcade was raised, the south aisle and chapel were being used as the nave and chancel, though arrangements were reversed to the present and presumably original state with the major restoration of 1895. The visitor will be amused by numerous lively corbel heads and gargoyles.

Sandy: St Swithun.

St Swithun's church, built in the fifteenth century, was totally restored in 1860. The roof of the Pym family vault was exposed in 1983 and is still visible. There is a fine statue of Sir William Peel (1824-58), who built his own private railway from Sandy to Potton and died of smallpox at Cawnpore in India. The Lady Chapel has been beautifully restored in memory of W. G. Braybrooks (died 1957) and his wife.

Sharnbrook: St Peter. (North of Bedford, just off A6.)

St Peter's is an attractive church with nave and aisles dating from the thirteenth century. The north chapel and tower were added a hundred years later. There is a large and conspicuous monument to the Magniac family of Colworth in the Tofte Chapel. Beside the tower in the graveyard is the monstrous

Magniac mausoleum, of the finest Victorian craftsmanship in coloured marble, and protected by a wooden shed.

Shelton: St Mary. (Between Rushden and St Neots, south of A45.)

St Mary's is surely the gem of Bedfordshire village churches. The light shines on uneven floor slabs, benches lean at odd angles, and everywhere is the simple work of the medieval country craftsman unaltered by major restorations. Externally it is fifteenth-century, but inside thirteenth- and fourteenth-century work survives. There are wall paintings and a fourteenth-century font on seven legs. Pews and chancel screen are local fifteenth-century products, polished with the patina of ages. Stuffed owls on the rafters are intended to scare away the bats. Outside are grotesque gargoyles and a clock with only one hand.

Shillington: All Saints. (North-west of Hitchin, west of A600.)

The dark sandstone and limestone of the church give it great dignity. The tower fell in 1701 and was not rebuilt for almost fifty years. Local legend still recalls the bells roll-

Early eighteenth-century gravestones in Potton churchyard.

*The delightfully
unrestored church of
St Mary at Shelton.*

ing down the hill to the stream. Inside is a great clerestoried hall, broken by the high chancel arch and aisles, built in the early fourteenth century. There is a crypt beneath the chancel. The church contains some fine wooden screens and is famous for a large brass to Matthew Asscheton, a canon of Lincoln, who died in 1400.

Southill: All Saints. (West of Biggleswade, west of B658.)

All Saints' church was rebuilt in brick and faced with cement in 1814-16, though the lower part of the tower and north aisle date from about 1300. The interior is rather plain, and only the clerestory reflects its Georgian date. There is a pleasant brick floor, and a number of wall monuments, including one to Edward Dilley, a local man who became a London bookseller and brought Samuel Johnson to the church. The Byng family vault

(not open) includes the tomb of Admiral John Byng, who was shot on board the flagship *Monarque* in 1757 (see page 102).

Stevington: St Mary. (North-west of Bedford, north of A428.)

St Mary's church has Saxon origins, visible in the long and short corner stones at the base of the tower, and in the narrow-arched Romanesque doorway leading into the south aisle. The belfry above is fourteenth-century, as are the clerestory, nave roof and screen in the tower arch. There is a good military brass of Thomas Salle (died 1422) and a great iron-bound parish chest. Carved on some of the bench ends are figures of boys seated, writing and drinking from bowls. Could the latter illustrate the village 'drinking' recorded in the sixteenth century, when the inhabitants beating the bounds reached Drinking Bush Hill and dug a hole, jumped into it and got drunk? At the foot of a high stone retaining wall to an original river terrace, to the east of the church, is a spring with old baptismal associations, always known as the Holy Wells.

Stotfold: St Mary. (North of Letchworth, bypassed by A507.)

This seems to have been a twelfth-century nave church, to which north and south aisles were later added, and a tower in the fifteenth century. The chancel dates from 1890. A fifteenth-century stair to the rood screen is entered from the north aisle. Little human heads are carved on the nave pillars. The font is of fourteenth-century date, and there are fragments of old glass in the central window of the north aisle. Wall paintings recorded in 1827 are no longer visible.

Sutton: All Saints. (North-east of Biggleswade, east of B1040.)

All Saints' church, built of the local ironstone and greensand pebbles, includes work of the thirteenth, fourteenth and fifteenth centuries. Corbels in the north aisle are decorated with a winged dragon and a cat playing a harp. There is a fine monument to Sir Roger Burgoyne (died 1677), lavishly decorated by Grinling Gibbons. In the gallery is a working Bates sacred barrel organ dated 1820 which plays thirty different hymn tunes. The Reverend Edward Drax Free (1765-1843) was prosecuted for lewdness, indecency and immorality, keeping pigs in the churchyard, fodder in the porch, and fighting with his clerk during a service.

Tempsford: St Peter. (North of Sandy, off A1.)

St Peter's church is built in brown and buff sandstone layers. Basically fourteenth-century, the interior suffered two drastic restorations in 1621 and 1874. The pulpit with its door is fifteenth-century. The east window contains good modern glass by Peter Bacon recalling Edward the Elder's defeat of the Danes at Tempsford in 921. There is an iron-bound parish chest carved from a single tree trunk. Wall monuments have been relegated to the inside of the tower, along with the kitchen sink.

Thurleigh: St Peter. (North of Bedford, between A6 and B660.)

A large neat graveyard surrounds St Peter's church. It is difficult to believe on entering this welcoming, light and airy church that the nave was derelict until 1976. The tower is twelfth-century Norman, and the nave was rebuilt in the fifteenth century. Over the south door of the tower is a carving of Adam and Eve, and opposite is an amusing notice for bellringers. The brass of a knight in armour on the nave floor recalls John Harvey, who died about 1420.

Tilsworth: All Saints. (South-east of Leighton Buzzard, west of A5.)

The church is mainly thirteenth-century and stands on a hilltop close to a poor motte and bailey castle earthwork. In the north aisle of the church are carved three thirteenth-century soldiers. There is also a tomb recess with the recumbent figure of a priest. Two good canopied tombs in the chancel are to Gabriel Fowler (died 1582) and Sir Henry Chester (died 1666). In the churchyard is a tombstone to a 'female unknown', a girl who was found in 1821 with her throat cut, lying against a tree in Blackgrove Wood.

Toddington: St George. (North of Dunstable, on A5120.)

St George's church was begun in the thirteenth century, but most of the work visible dates from the fourteenth and fifteenth centuries and the 1876 restoration. The friable Totternhoe stone on the exterior has caused many problems and some of it has recently been restored: a delightful frieze of sixteenth-century animals includes a sow and piglets, the original of the nearby pub name. Inside, the high nave of the early fourteenth century has an excellent roof decorated with angels. The north transept forms the sixteenth-century Wentworth Chapel and contains a monument to Lady Henrietta Wentworth. The Cheyne Chapel recalls the Cheyne family, one of whom entertained Elizabeth I at the original manor. Their badly mutilated monuments remind us that in the eighteenth and early nineteenth centuries the church was in ruins. On the north side of the chancel is a three-storeyed vestry which was used as a priest's house.

Turvey: All Saints. (West of Bedford, on A428.)

All Saints' church is a joy. Thomas of Leighton's thirteenth-century ironwork on the south door is an indication of pleasures to come. The tower and south aisles show traces of Saxon work. The south and north aisles were thirteenth- and fifteenth-century additions respectively. In an alcove in the south aisle is a very fine early fourteenth-century wall painting of the Crucifixion. George Gilbert Scott's restoration of 1854 has made Turvey the finest mid-Victorian example of what the Oxford Movement stood for in Bedfordshire. Surviving from earlier times are four dramatic monuments, three with recumbent figures, to members of the Mordant family, whose home stood at Hall Farm.

Woburn: St Mary. (North-east of Leighton Buzzard, on A4012.)

New St Mary's church, built (1865-8) of Bath stone by Henry Clutton for the eighth Duke of Bedford, is a grand building in a late twelfth-century French style, which visitors will either love or hate. No expense has been spared. It should certainly be seen. Beneath it is a crypt sometimes used for exhibitions.

Yelden: St Mary. (East of Rushden, north-east of A6.)

A large castle earthwork dominates the east side of this tiny village (see page 62), and St Mary's stands sentinel on the west. The main nave and chancel walls of the church were built about 1220, although the building was remodelled in 1340 and the south aisle widened around that time. The tower is not very much later and outside has a pleasing frieze of leaves, animals and leering heads below the eaves of the spire. The interior is light and airy, with two tomb recesses in the nave walls. One on the south contains an early fourteenth-century male figure holding his heart. The more elaborate southern recess is empty. In the tower is a curious lead inscription, written in dialect by Thomas Williamson, dated 1700.

William Dell was rector in the seventeenth century. A puritan and Master of Caius College, Cambridge, he allowed John Bunyan to preach in the church on Christmas Day 1659. His parishioners objected, and in 1662 he was ejected from Yelden and retired to Westoning, where he died soon afterwards and was buried in unconsecrated ground at Lower Samshill.

An avenue of limes leads to Hulcote church.

Stockgrove Country Park.

6
Historic buildings and gardens

All the buildings and gardens described here are open to the public, but some for only a restricted period during the summer. Visitors are advised to check the times of opening before making a journey.

Avenue House, 20 Church Street, Ampthill, Bedford MK45 2EH. National Trust covenanted property.
Open by appointment in June and July. Applications in writing to Simon Houfe at Avenue House.
The home of the architect Sir Albert Richardson from June 1919 until his death in 1964, this country-town house was built for John Morris, the local brewer, designed by the Bedford architect John Wing in the 1780s and enlarged by him in 1819. Described as 'a microcosm of Regency living', by good fortune and with loving care it has survived almost unchanged to the present day. This is not a museum but a time capsule with direct access to the past. There is a large garden, designed in keeping with the house, containing original features.

Bromham Mill, Bromham, Bedford. Telephone: 01234 824330. Bedfordshire County Council. Situated at the western end of Bromham Bridge, together with a picnic site and nature reserve.
Open: April to October, daily except Mondays and Tuesdays, but open bank holidays.
Built of stone and brick, the mill stands beside the river Great Ouse. The oldest parts of the surviving building are those nearest to the river, dated 1695 and 1722. The western section was added in 1858. There were originally two undershot wooden waterwheels, neither of which survive. The single iron breast wheel which replaced the smaller of the two in 1908 has been restored to working

order, driving two pairs of Derby peak stones. The mill now belongs to the Bedfordshire County Council and is open to the public in summer as a museum, incorporating various display areas, an arts and crafts gallery and natural history room. Milling demonstrations are held on the last Sunday of each month and bank holiday Mondays.

Bushmead Priory, near Colmworth, Bedford MK44 2LD. Telephone: 01230 62614 or 01703 557031. English Heritage.
Open: July to August, weekends only.
St Mary's Priory, Bushmead, was founded by William, chaplain of Colmworth, in 1195. Some twenty years later the Augustinian rule was adopted. Following the Dissolution in 1536, only the refectory and parts of the kitchen and north-east corner of the cloister survive. These were converted into a mansion by the Gery family who still occupy it. Visitors will see the canons' refectory with its magnificent roof, a rare example of crownpost construction, dating from about 1250. There are early fourteenth-century wall paintings and later stained glass. Close by is the timbered Old Brew House.

Chicksands Priory, RAF Chicksands, Shefford. Telephone: 01462 852226 (Monday to Friday); 01234 824195 (weekends).
Open: April to October, first and third Sunday afternoons each month.
The priory was founded in about 1150 by Payne de Beauchamp and his wife, the Countess Rohese, for a mixed community of monks and nuns of the Gilbertine order. After the Dissolution it passed into the hands of the Snowe family, then in 1576 to Peter Osborne. His great granddaughter Dorothy (page 103) is best remembered for her love letters to William Temple, written between 1652 and

1654. Today part of the building is cement-rendered, and nineteenth-century Gothic in appearance. The main rooms are largely the work of Isaac Ware in 1740, with the entrance hall, main stair and domestic wing dating from James Wyatt in 1813. Its recent history under various government departments has been sad, with much minor damage and poor decoration. Fortunately the Friends of the Priory are working to restore it. In the eastern entrance hall is a wall inscription recalling the Priory's ghost, a fallen nun called Rosata, who, on being found pregnant, is supposed to have been walled up alive in the cloister. The Haynes Grange room in the Victoria and Albert Museum is said to have come from the Priory but this is open to doubt. At the back of the house is an outside larder with ceiling hooks for the meat, and close by can be seen the Orangery of about 1800.

The de Grey Mausoleum, Flitton, Bedford. English Heritage. Keyholder: Mr Stimpson, 3 Highfield Road, Flitton. Telephone: 01525 860094.
Open at weekends.

The mausoleum is entered from the chancel of the church of St John. It was begun as a chapel about 1614, with an addition in 1705. It is the burial place of the de Grey family of Wrest Park at Silsoe. The earliest monument is a brass to Henry Gray (died 1545). Most dominant is the tomb of Henry Grey, fifth Earl of Kent (died 1614), and his wife, Mary, with their reclining figures carved from alabaster and brightly painted. The tomb of the ninth Earl, Henry (died 1651), and his wife, Amabel, the 'Good Countess', is carved from white marble. There are monuments to the children of the first Duke of Kent, almost all of whom died young. The most elegant monument is to the first Duke himself, and his two wives. It was designed and signed by Edward Shepherd about 1730. The highly sensitive Victorian monument to Henrietta Frances, Countess de Grey, who died in 1848, shows a weeping husband and family and an angel carrying her soul to heaven. Visiting the mausoleum in 1789, the diarist John Byng was not altogether impressed: 'The old recumbent figures of Henry, Earl of Kent, and his Countess,

are very fine; but those of a later date are abominable: a son of the last Duke, a lad, in a Wig, and a Shirt! The Duke himself, upon a cumb'rous monument, as a Roman, with his English ducal cap!'

Houghton House, Ampthill, Bedford. English Heritage.
Open at any reasonable time.

Built of orange-red brick and Totternhoe stone, this haunting ruin is one of the most evocative places in Bedfordshire. It was built for the Countess of Pembroke in 1615, and after her death in 1621 it became the home of the Earls of Ailesbury. It was bought in 1738 by the Duke of Bedford, and his son the Marquess of Tavistock lived there from 1764 until his death three years later in a tragic riding accident. In 1794 the Duke had it demolished. A staircase of 1688 is now in the Swan Hotel, Bedford, and early eighteenth-century gates from the park are in Church Street, Ampthill. Houghton House is tradi-

The ruins of Houghton House overlooking the Vale of Bedford.

St Margaret's church, Higham Gobion.

St Mary's Priory at Bushmead.

The roofless nave of Segenhoe Old Church, near Ridgmont.

The Dining Room at Luton Hoo.

tionally John Bunyan's Palace Beautiful, which Christian reached by climbing the Hill Difficulty. The view from the ruin on a fine day is one of the best in the county.

Luton Hoo, Luton LU1 3TQ. Telephone: 01582 22955.
Open: April to October, daily except Mondays, but open on bank holidays.

The mansion was begun in 1767 by Robert Adam for the third Earl of Bute, who was at that time an undistinguished Prime Minister and is better remembered as a naturalist. The 1500 acre (607 hectare) park was laid out at the same time by 'Capability' Brown. After a series of fires the house was remodelled in 1903 by Mewes and Davis, architects of the Ritz hotels in London and Paris, for Sir Julius Wernher, a diamond magnate. The most pleasing part of the interior is possibly the oval staircase hall in the French Beaux Arts style. The house contains the Wernher collec-

tion of paintings, tapestries and furniture, medieval ivories and English porcelain. The Russian collection includes many jewelled objects by Fabergé. The formal and rock gardens are also open to the public. Luton Hoo has provided the setting for numerous films, including *Four Weddings and a Funeral.*

Segenhoe Old Church, Ridgmont, Bedford. Bedfordshire County Council.
Open at any reasonable time.

All Saints' church was considered unfashionable by the Duke of Bedford, who built a replacement in 1854 in the village of Ridgmont. The old church lingered on for another seventy years, after which it was abandoned, although part of the graveyard remained in use. By 1972 it was overgrown and ruined. Clearance and preservation work by the County Council in the 1980s has produced a fascinating, yet little-known architectural monument. The original church of chancel and aisleless nave probably dated from the early twelfth century. The nave was extended, a north aisle added in stages and a south aisle commenced but abandoned by the fourteenth century. Between 1823 and 1826 the north aisle was heightened and the tower added (to replace a small bellcote) and the whole exterior of the building was given a rendering of cement to produce a classical Georgian church. Decay has been halted at a stage which enables the fabric of the church and its rebuilds to be seen clearly, so it is possible to deduce the architectural history of the building with various intriguing alternatives: it is a superb puzzle in vertical stratigraphy.

Someries Castle, Hyde, near Luton. Bedfordshire County Council. Best approached from Chiltern Green.
Open at any reasonable time.

In spite of its name, Someries Castle was a prestige building, designed to impress, and not for military strength. A gatehouse and adjoining chapel are all that remain today of a much larger house, which stood to the south, built by John, Lord Wenlock, about 1448. These are the earliest brick buildings in the county and very little stone has been incorpo-

rated. The ruined gatehouse consists of an entrance passageway flanked by two massive part-octagonal turrets. The western one has a pedestrian passageway passing through it and also contained a garderobe. A newel staircase in the south-west corner of the ruin, entirely constructed from brick, led to the upper floor and to a cellar, now filled in. The chapel to the east was added a few years later, probably after Wenlock's attainder for treason had been annulled in 1460. An inventory of 1606 referred to twenty-one rooms as well as farm buildings but most of these were pulled down by John Napier in 1742. There is no truth in stories of an underground passage to Luton parish church. To the south-west are earthworks, possibly of an earlier house, pulled down by Wenlock, or more probably they may be gardens for the later house. The novelist Joseph Conrad lived for a time in the adjoining farmhouse.

Stevington Post Mill, Stevington, Bedford. Bedfordshire County Council. Telephone: 01234 822184.
Key from the Royal George Inn, Silver Street, Stevington.

One of the crosstrees inside the windmill is inscribed 1770, and this probably dates the

The gatehouse of Someries Castle, one of the earliest brick buildings in England.

Stevington Mill, restored for the Festival of Britain in 1951.

building. It was almost certainly built for Richard Pool, who was miller in the village in 1778. Its body was entirely rebuilt in 1921 and did not copy the original. It went out of use about 1936. In 1951 the Bedfordshire County Council acquired it and restored it to working order. It is the only surviving post mill in the county and was probably the last mill in Britain to have four 'common' (cloth-covered) sails. These were the earliest kind of sails and it was necessary to reef them by hand according to the varying winds. The roundhouse, built of limestone and roofed with orange tile, was added in the nineteenth century.

The Swiss Garden, Old Warden, Biggleswade. Telephone: 01767 627666 or 01234 228330. Bedfordshire County Council. *Open: April to October, daily except Tuesdays; January to March, Sunday only.*

It was Robert, third Lord Ongley of Old Warden, who created The Swiss Garden in the 1820s. The design of the romantic *jardin ornée* was at its height, and it seems likely that J. B. Papworth, author of *Hints on Ornamental Gardening* (1823), may have advised

him. After years of neglect it was taken into the County Council's care in 1976 and is being painstakingly restored. Visitors will need to purchase the guide-map to appreciate the finer points. Today the garden is fully matured and surprise views through the trees are one of its delights. Noteworthy are the Grotto and Swiss Cottage. The former, cleverly created from tufa stone, leads into the glass and cast-iron Fernery. One wonders how the curved window glass was cut without breaking. The Swiss Cottage on its rounded hill is the centrepiece of the garden. A thatched tree shelter has an inscribed stone beside it carrying Lord Ongley's poem to a childhood friend. Although resources are limited, with time this garden will live again, but it is a landscaped garden: do not expect neat 'municipal' flower beds.

Willington Dovecote and Stables, Willington, Bedford. National Trust. Telephone: 01234 838278.
Open: April to September, by appointment only.

Sir John Gostwick bought the manor of Willington in 1529 and, since it was a lord's privilege to keep pigeons to provide him with fresh meat in the winter, he had the dovecote built soon afterwards. It is a tall narrow stone building with a two-tiered tiled roof with stepped gables at each end. Two low doors lead into separate compartments which between them have nesting boxes for about 1500 birds. Some of the stone for the dovecote may have come from Newnham Priory near Bedford, including a gargoyle high in the stable rafters. Across the road is the so-called 'King Henry's Stables', built by Gostwick in the same style with stepped gables, buttresses, mullioned windows and large entrance. A modern staircase leads to the loft, which has a fireplace and provides a good view of the roof timbers. Glass protects the graffiti signature of John Bunyan. The style of lettering suggests that this is probably genuine.

Opposite: *The Swiss Garden at Old Warden was created in the 1820s by Robert, third Lord Ongley, and has been restored by Bedfordshire County Council.*

Woburn Abbey, Woburn MK43 0TP. Telephone: 01525 290666.
Open: January to March, weekends only; April to October daily. Closed: November to December.

Woburn Abbey was founded as a Cistercian monastery in 1145 and prospered until its destruction by fire in the sixteenth century. The remains were granted to John Russell, later first Earl of Bedford, in the will of Henry VIII in 1547. The fourth Earl rebuilt the house about 1630, incorporating a little medieval fabric in the north range. The new building followed the rectangular plan of the monastery, as did subsequent rebuildings until 1950, when the east wing was demolished because of dry rot. Amongst numerous architects employed at Woburn, Henry Flitcroft (1747-61) and Henry Holland (1787-90) are probably the most important. Flitcroft designed the West Front, Stable Courts and the State Rooms. Much of Holland's work disappeared during the demolition of 1950, but the Library, Canaletto Room and other rooms in the south wing survive, as do the Chinese Dairy and Sculpture Gallery outside the house.

Visitors will have their own favourite exhibits amongst the great display of furniture, paintings, sculpture and ceramics, and it would be invidious to select individual items, which include Van Dycks, Rembrandts, Canalettos and porcelain and silver of the highest quality. A lot of the pictures in the house will be familiar to visitors as they have been reproduced many times.

To the east of the house and raised above it, a magnificent cedar tree separates two stable blocks, which now house an antiques centre and restaurant. Much of the park was remodelled by Humphry Repton in the early nineteenth century. Its greatest pleasure lies in the mature trees and large herds of wandering deer. The Woburn Safari Park (see page 99) is unobtrusive in the northern area.

Wrest Park, Silsoe, Bedford MK45 4HS. Telephone: 01525 860125 or 860178. Silsoe Research Institute with English Heritage.
Open: April to September, weekends and bank holidays.

From 1284 the manor of Wrest was held by Reginald de Grey and it remained with his descendants for six hundred years. Lord Grey of Ruthin was created Earl of Kent by Edward IV. The original house stood 200 metres (220 yards) to the south of the present building.

Henry Flitcroft designed the west front of Woburn Abbey.

The south front of Wrest Park, designed by Philip, second Earl de Grey.

Between 1834 and 1839 Thomas Philip, second Earl de Grey, and first President of the Institute of British Architects, pulled down the old house and built the present mansion. He was both architect and builder. The style is essentially French throughout and is so successful that Professor Pevsner was deceived into believing it to have been the work of a French architect. The principal rooms are on the ground floor looking south over the gardens. Most of the decoration is in white and gold. The ceilings were painted by John Wood, and the bas-reliefs were by Smith from rough sketches by the Earl, who 'personally enhanced the charms of some of the ladies depicted'. Visitors see state rooms, including the entrance hall, library, and dining and drawing rooms.

The glory of Wrest is the garden laid out by Henry Grey, Duke of Kent, from 1706 to 1740, and twenty years later modified by Jemima, Marchioness de Grey, with the professional assistance of 'Capability' Brown. The formal lines of the Great Garden were softened by separating the encircling canals and making minor changes which did little damage to the original design. From the terrace one passes Dutch lead statues, a marble fountain, and statues copied from originals in the Vatican. The Long Water was probably dug about 1680. At its extremity stands Thomas Archer's Pavilion of 1711, a rare example of English baroque, with its internal *trompe l'oeil* painting by Hauduroy. Tiny staircases lead down to the kitchen and water closet and up to what was the servants' accommodation. Other garden buildings include the Orangery (1836), where refreshments may be obtained, the Bowling Green House (1735) and the restored Chinese Pavilion.

7
Museums and art galleries

Bedford

Bedford Museum, Castle Lane, Bedford MK40 3XD. Telephone: 01234 353323.
Open: Tuesday to Sunday, except Good Friday and Christmas.

Opened in 1981 in a converted brewery, the collections had first been gathered together in the late nineteenth century by Charles Prichard. The displays are still growing and it is possible to see objects illustrating nineteenth-century rural life, including a reconstructed labourer's cottage living room, a farmhouse kitchen and a dairy. On the first floor the displays illustrate the development of Bedford as a community and the county's geology, natural history and archaeology. Here can be seen the museum's greatest treasures, the Celtic mirror from Old Warden and the bronzes from Felmersham. There is usually a temporary exhibition on the ground floor, and there is a well-stocked publications stall.

Bunyan Meeting Museum and Library, Mill Street, Bedford MK40 3EU. Telephone: 01234 358870 or 212485.
Open: April to October, Tuesday to Saturday afternoons.

The museum is believed to contain all the surviving personal relics of John Bunyan and the world's largest collection of copies of *The Pilgrim's Progress*, in 168 languages. The original volume of the church book can be seen containing many entries in Bunyan's handwriting. His chair, fiddle, anvil, cabinet, jug and walking stick are also in the museum. Small exhibitions are held in the library. In the adjoining meeting house is the stained glass window that inspired Terry Waite when he was incarcerated in Beirut. (Bedford Public Library also houses a collection of Bunyan's works and related publications.)

Opposite: *Elstow Moot Hall and church.*

Cecil Higgins Art Gallery and Museum,
Castle Close, Bedford MK40 3NY. Telephone: 01234 211222.
Open: Tuesday to Saturday, and Sunday afternoons; closed Christmas, Boxing Day and Good Friday.

The Cecil Higgins Art Gallery and Museum combines the original home of the Higgins family, now displayed as a furnished Victorian house, with an award-winning extension built in 1974.

The Victorian house is arranged in room settings to evoke the 'lived-in' atmosphere of a well-to-do family home. The ground floor includes a drawing room, dining room and library, and the first floor has a guest bedroom, a nursery and a bedroom with furniture designed by the famous Victorian architect William Burges.

The modern extension has changing exhibitions of its internationally important collection of watercolours, including works by Turner, Constable and Gainsborough, and a fine collection of prints by leading artists such as Rembrandt, the Impressionists and Picasso. There are permanent displays of English and European ceramics and glass and a fine collection of English and foreign lace is also on display; nineteenth-century Bedfordshire lace is particularly well represented.

St Mary's Church Archaeology Centre, St Mary's Street, Bedford. Telephone: 01234 270002.
Open: weekdays only, late morning and mid afternoon.

This is the headquarters of the County Planning Department's Archaeology Service. Display panels illustrate the work of the Department.

Elstow

Elstow Moot Hall, Church Lane, Elstow, Bedford MK42 9XT. Telephone: 01234 266889.

Tureen in the form of a hen with her chicks, Chelsea, c.1755, in the Cecil Higgins Art Gallery.

Open: April to October, Tuesday, Thursday, Saturday and Sunday afternoons.

A market house of the late fifteenth or early sixteenth century, of timber-frame construction and orange brick, carefully restored in 1951, the Moot Hall stands on the village green and would have been used in connection with markets and fairs. The large open hall on the first floor was the scene of parish meetings. The Moot Hall contains a permanent exhibition illustrating English seventeenth-century life and traditions associated with the life of John Bunyan, who grew up in the village. There is a particularly fine display of furniture, and early editions of Bunyan's books.

Luton

John Dony Field Centre, Hancock Drive, Bushmead, Luton LU2 7SF. Telephone: 01582 486983.
Open: Monday to Friday, and Sunday mornings.

Housed at the Bushmead Community Centre, the Field Centre was opened in 1990. It contains natural history displays, focusing on the conservation of sites of natural history interest in the Luton district. There is also a wildlife garden and an education/meeting room for use by school and other educational groups, along with changing exhibitions in the summer months.

Luton Museum and Art Gallery, Wardown Park, Old Bedford Road, Luton LU2 7HA. Telephone: 01582 746723.
Open daily.

Housed in a small Victorian mansion built in 1875 and set within a park, this is the museum of Luton and south Bedfordshire. It contains extensive collections of local archaeology, natural history, costume, Bedfordshire lacemaking, hatmaking, and a local history archive. There is also a children's gallery and there are relics of the Bedfordshire and Hertfordshire Regiment. The museum's greatest treasure is the Register of the Fraternity of Luton, a beautifully illustrated manuscript book of the mid fifteenth and sixteenth centuries. A reconstructed pillow lacemaker's sitting room has long been a popular exhibit, as have displays of Luton's hat trade. There is a programme of changing exhibitions in the Art Gallery. Numerous publications and other souvenirs are on sale in the gift shop. There are facilities for visitors with disabilities and refreshments are available.

Stockwood Craft Museum and Gardens and Mossman Collection, Stockwood Country Park, Farley Hill, Luton LU1 4BH. Telephone: 01582 38714 or 746723.
Open: April to October, Tuesday to Sunday and bank holidays; November to March, weekends.

Stockwood House was built by John Crawley in 1740 and demolished in 1964, only the red-brick stable block remaining. This now houses the Craft Museum opened in 1986 and collections include the Bedfordshire crafts and rural trades items amassed by Thomas W. Bagshawe earlier in the twentieth century. Amongst the exhibits are a reconstructed working forge from Toddington, carpenter's, saddler's and cobbler's workshops, rushwork, basketwork and straw plait, together with agricultural implements and photographs. Live craft demonstrations take place most weekends, and adjoining are a walled

Victorian garden and other period gardens, including the Ian Hamilton Finlay sculpture garden. There is a sales counter in a reconstructed timber-framed building at the entrance. There are also facilities for visitors with disabilities, and refreshments are available in the Conservatory Tea Room.

Also at Stockwood Craft Museum is the Mossman Collection, a modern purpose-built museum housing over seventy original and replica horse-drawn vehicles, from carriages to carts, together with the collection of the Hackney Horse Society Museum, and vintage motors from the Chiltern Vehicle Preservation Society. Pride of place goes to an early nineteenth-century mail coach, the 'Old Times', which ran from London to Brighton and back in eight hours.

Old Warden
The Shuttleworth Collection, Old Warden Aerodrome, Biggleswade SG18 9ER. Telephone: 01767 627288.
Open daily, but closed Christmas Eve to New Year's Day inclusive.

Housed in a group of purpose-built hangars beside a classic active grass aerodrome, this collection of aeroplanes and cars was begun by Richard Ormonde Shuttleworth in 1928.

The 1910 Deperdussin taking off from Old Warden aerodrome.

The walled Victorian garden at Stockwood Craft Museum, Luton.

The collection illustrates the history of aviation with flyable veteran aeroplanes ranging from the Blériot Type XI of 1909 to a 1942 Spitfire. There is a great variety of machines which one can see in close-up detail, as well as being able to watch many of them fly on the museum's frequent open days. There are also fascinating relics of the great airships. In the workshops aeroplanes can be seen undergoing routine maintenance and reconstruction. There are also veteran cars, motorcycles, bicycles and horse-drawn carriages. There is a well-stocked souvenir shop and restaurant, a children's playground and a large picnic parking area.

Stondon

Transport Museum and Garden Centre, Station Road, Lower Stondon, Henlow SG16 6JN. Telephone: 01462 850339.
Open daily.

This wide-ranging collection of mainly twentieth-century vehicles is in course of development. Three halls are at present open and contain veteran and vintage cars and motorcycles, and more than a hundred classic cars. Utility and Second World War vehicles, farm tractors and equipment, public transport and aircraft are all represented in the collection, and some of these will be demonstrated on an adjoining track. Replicas of Captain James Cook's ship, the *Endeavour*, and Stephenson's *Rocket* should be in place during 1995.

Woburn

Woburn Heritage Centre, St Mary's Old Church, 9 Bedford Street, Woburn. Contact address: 1 Leighton Street, Woburn, Milton Keynes MK17 9PJ. Telephone: 01525 290631.
Open: May to October, Monday to Friday afternoons, Saturdays and Sundays.

This small museum illustrates the history of Woburn village from Saxon times to the present day and is housed in a mortuary chapel built in 1865. It stands on the site of old St Mary's church, of which only the base of the medieval tower, redesigned by Blore in 1830, survives. It contains an unfinished alabaster monument to Sir Francis and Dame Elizabeth Staunton (died 1630).

8
Other places to visit

Airship Sheds, Shortstown, Cardington, Bedford. Clearly visible from the A600 parking places.

In 1917 Short Brothers began to build a factory and shed for the manufacture of airships. The northern shed is 247.5 metres (812 feet) long, 118.5 metres (389 feet) wide and 54.9 metres (180 feet) high. It consists of twenty-nine bays of steel framing, with aisles along each side and a massive central nave. Its enormous doors each weigh 940 tons and are opened by electric motors. It was built to house the government-sponsored R101 airship. The southern shed was brought to Cardington from Norfolk and erected in 1928 for the privately built R100. It is the same size as the earlier shed. In 1930 the R101 crashed near Beauvais in France on her maiden voyage. Only six of its fifty-four passengers and crew survived. As a result airship production ceased. For a time the sheds were used for storing aircraft and barrage balloons, parachute training and even rehearsing the Royal Tournament. The Airship Museum is at present closed and looking for a new home.

Leighton Buzzard Railway, Page's Park Station, Billington Road, Leighton Buzzard LU7 8TN. Telephone: 01525 373888.
Open: April to October, Sundays; and bank holidays. Telephone for details.

This narrow-gauge railway was built in 1919 to carry sand from quarries north of the town south to the main London & North Western Railway line at Grovebury. At its peak it was carrying 3000 tons of sand each week. In the late 1960s the commercial life of the line was coming to an end, but a group of railway enthusiasts formed a preservation society. On 3rd March 1968 the first passenger train of the new society ran to Double Arches and back. Since then the track has been rebuilt and twelve steam and thirty-eight diesel locomotives acquired, some from as far away as India and West Africa. A return journey of 5½ miles (9 km) takes an hour from Page's Park in Billington Road, where there is ample car parking, a souvenir shop and buffet.

Leighton Lady Cruises, Brantom's Wharf, Canal Side, Leighton Buzzard LU7 3BR.

The Airship Sheds at Cardington.

The Leighton Buzzard Railway picking up passengers at Page's Park.

Telephone: 01525 384563.

Boat trips on the Grand Union Canal are available on bank holidays and in August, and private charters throughout the year.

London Luton International Airport, Luton. Telephone: 01582 405100.

This is the fourth busiest airport and the leading charter holiday flight airport in Britain. It handles 1.9 million passengers every year and thousands of tons of freight. It is dominated by the tallest control tower in Britain. This opened in 1995 and is 164 feet (50 metres) high. There is a viewing enclosure from which visitors may watch aircraft landing and taking off.

Melchbourne Bird Gardens, Vicarage Farm, Knotting Road, Melchbourne MK44 1BQ. Telephone: 01234 708317.
Open daily.

This is one of the finest displays of pheasants in England, together with waterfowl, geese and other birds. All the specimens have been bred in Britain, and some, surplus to requirements, can be purchased. There is a picnic area and limited refreshments.

Toddington Manor Rare Breeds Centre, Toddington LU5 6HJ. Telephone: 01525 872576.
Open: Easter Saturday to end of September, daily.

Situated in the beautiful grounds of the manor, the remnant of an Elizabethan house, the well-stocked centre has pedigree herds of White Park, Longhorn and Highland cattle, together with flocks of Portland, black Hebridean and rare Norfolk Horn sheep. There are also rare pigs and poultry. The gardens, woods and lakes are accessible to visitors though sometimes muddy, and there is an enormous collection of vintage farm machinery, including more than a hundred European and North American tractors. During the season visitors can see sheep shearing, lamb feeding, spinning and machinery demonstrations and enjoy vintage tractor rides. There is an excellent tea room with home-made produce and an attractive shop.

Whipsnade Wild Animal Park, Whipsnade, Dunstable LU6 2LF. Telephone: 01582 872171.
Open daily except Christmas Day.

England's most famous zoo was opened on 23rd May 1931. Just over 570 acres (230 hectares) of downland provide a magnificent setting for the Zoological Society of London's country park, which commands extensive views from the chalk escarpment into south Bedfordshire and Buckinghamshire.

The spaciousness of Whipsnade is impressive, particularly in spring when the cherry trees provide a broad avenue of blossom and the woods are full of bluebells. Whipsnade is generally the home of the society's larger mammals, whilst the smaller ones, requiring temperature-controlled houses, are kept in London. Not only are there popular favourites like elephants, chimpanzees, bears, lions, tigers, rhinoceros and penguins, but one can also see some of the world's most endangered species, such as the Indian rhinoceros, the red panda (as rare as its more famous black and white cousin), the Nile lechwe and Przewalski horse. There are a number of free-roaming animals, including the Chinese water deer and muntjac, and the more unusual wallabies and mara (a type of South American guinea pig). Walking quietly on the edge of the downs, you may spot the prairie marmots in their colony.

All year round there are regular sea-lion and free-flying birds of the world demonstrations and elephant encounters. The Discovery Centre allows children a close-up view of smaller species such as snakes, frogs and fish. The Run Wild Play Centre and BP Bear Maze cater for smaller children. The park offers winter saver prices and discounts for parties. It has a restaurant, snack bars, ample picnic areas and a well-stocked gift shop.

Woburn Safari Park, Woburn, Milton Keynes. Telephone: 01525 290407.
Open: mid March to October, daily.

300 acres (20 hectares) of parkland form the largest drive-through safari park in Britain. Wild animals have been kept at Woburn for over a hundred years. Now they are easily available for all to see. The different species are impressive: elephants, lions, tigers, rhinoceroses, bears and many others. Motorists can drive through the paddocks with the fiercest animals at liberty outside the window. In the adjoining leisure area there is a display of sea-lions and parrots, and elephants at work, as well as the Adventure Ark, Pen-

Longhorn cattle at Toddington Manor Rare Breeds Centre.

Rhinoceros at Whipsnade Wild Animal Park.

guin World and boating lakes. There is a restaurant and gift shop and ample picnic space.

Woodside Farm and Wildlife Park, Mancroft Road, Aley Green, Slip End, Luton LU1 4DG. Telephone: 01582 841044.

Open all the year, except Sundays.
Set in 6¹/₂ acres (2.6 hectares), just off the A5, this collection of pure and rare breeds also offers a children's farm, tractor-trailor rides, pony rides, waterfowl area, farm shop and the Coffee Pot café. There is a large indoor rabbit warren.

9
Famous people

Although many famous people have had associations with Bedfordshire, remarkably few have lived there for more than a year or two. The medieval composer **John Dunstable** (*c.*1390-1453) may have been born in the county. He was employed by John, Duke of Bedford, the brother of Henry V. The poet **John Donne** probably spent a little time at Blunham, where he was rector from 1622. Bedford-born **Mark Rutherford** (actually William Hale White, 1831-1913) was a minor Victorian novelist, overshadowed by **Arnold Bennett** (1863-1931), who lived at Trinity Hall Farm, Hockliffe, for two years, and **Joseph Conrad** (1857-1924) at Someries Farm, Luton. **H. E. Bates** (1905-74) was born at Rushden in Northamptonshire, but his most famous creation, Uncle Silas, lived over the border in north Bedfordshire. The poet and playright **Christopher Fry** (born 1907) attended Bedford School, as did the Olympic gold medalist in the 100 metres of 1924, **Harold Abrahams**, subject of the film *Chariots of Fire*. The film actor **Gary Cooper**

Robert Bloomfield.

(1901-61) was educated at Dunstable Grammar School, whilst the American bandleader **Glenn Miller** flew to his death from Twin Woods airfield near Clapham in 1944. The architect and President of the Royal Academy **Sir Albert Richardson** (1880-1964) lived at Avenue House, Ampthill, from 1919 until his death. The Luton-born local historian and botanist **John Dony** (1899-1991), President of the Botanical Society of the British Isles, spent his whole life working and writing about the county. His mentor **Sir Frederick Mander** (1883-1964) was also Luton-born. He rose from schoolteacher to become General Secretary of the National Union of Teachers and chairman of the County Council.

Robert Bloomfield (1766-1823)

A minor poet of the countryside, Robert Bloomfield lived at Shefford from 1812 until his death, when he was buried at Campton. Born on 3rd December 1766 at Honington in Suffolk, he was a sickly child and at fifteen joined his elder brothers in London as a shoemaker's apprentice. He began writing poetry in his early twenties and by the age of thirty-two he was ready to publish *The Farmer's Boy*, a considerable achievement for a country boy with no formal education. It appeared in March 1800 and by the end of the year had reached its third edition. Whilst in London he produced much poetry and was well patronised. In 1790 he had married Mary Anne Church and they had five children. The family moved to Shefford when Robert was forty-five. Little poetry was written in Bedfordshire. He became ill and almost totally blind and his wife's mental illness added to their problems. His financial state became critical and he died on 18th August 1823.

John Bunyan (1628-88)

John Bunyan was born in a cottage near Harrowden in Elstow parish in 1628, the son of a brazier or tinker. As a child he accompanied his father on visits to Houghton House near Ampthill (the Palace Beautiful); in the distance they saw the Chiltern Hills at Sharpenhoe (the Delectable Mountains), and going east they passed through the marshy Soul's Slough near Tempsford (the Slough of Despond). He was taught to read and write, learned his father's profession and enjoyed his leisure time in playing and dancing on the village green (Vanity Fair). At nineteen he served in the Parliamentary army at Newport Pagnell for a brief time. On his return to Elstow he resumed his father's trade and soon afterwards married a local girl, by whom he had four children, including blind Mary. It was at about this time that he began to experience deep religious feelings and realised that life had a far greater purpose. The young family moved to Bedford, where John made the acquaintance of John Gifford, an Independent pastor of St John's church in Bedford. They were soon close friends and before long Bunyan was preaching to local Independent congregations and writing his first book attacking Quakerism. In 1659, after the death of his first wife, he married a girl called Elizabeth. In November 1660 he was arrested whilst preaching at Lower Samshill near Westoning and was committed to the old Bedford prison at the corner of Silver Street and High Street, where he remained for twelve years. Whilst there he wrote a number of religious tracts including *The Holy City* and *Grace Abounding*. With the Declaration of Indulgence of 1672 he was released and became a licensed preacher leading the Independent congregation in a barn in Mill Street, Bedford. In 1676, the Declaration having been cancelled, Bunyan was again sent to prison for six months. Whilst there he wrote the first part of *The Pilgrim's Progress*, published in 1678 for 1s 6d. A sequel appeared in 1685. His later life was divided between preaching in Bedford and many other parts of Britain and in writing more than sixty books, amongst them *The Life and Death of Mr Badman* (1680) and *The Holy War* (1682). After riding in the rain from Reading to London in August 1688 he caught a chill and died in Holborn, being buried in Bunhill Fields, London.

Admiral John Byng (1704-57)

John (Jack) Byng was born at Southill on 28th October 1704, the fourth son of George, first Viscount Torrington. He joined the navy at fourteen and rose to become an admiral in the Mediterranean command. In 1756 he was sent to relieve the French blockade of Minorca but failed to do so. Popular anger was directed at Byng, and his brother-in-law, Sir Henry Osborne of Chicksands Priory, was sent to arrest him. He was court-martialled at Portsmouth, and though he was acquitted of cowardice he was found guilty of neglect of duty and condemned to death. He was shot on the quarterdeck of the *Monarque*. He was buried in Southill church. The French writer Voltaire summed up the incident by writing: 'the English find it pays to shoot an admiral from time to time to encourage the others.'

John Byng, fifth Viscount Torrington (1743-1813)

John was the youngest son of George, third Viscount Torrington. He was educated at Westminster School. He became a page to George II and then entered the army as a cornet in the Royal Horse Guards. He retired from the first Foot Guards with the rank of Lieutenant-Colonel in 1780. He then joined the Inland Revenue at Somerset House. 'His early days were spent in Camps, his latter days were pass'd at Stamps', he wrote of himself. We have no details of his quarrel with his elder brother, George, the fourth Viscount. It was during the years 1781 to 1794 that he wrote his diaries, which give such graphic details of east Bedfordshire life in the late eighteenth century. In 1812 his brother died, but not before he had sold the Southill estate to Samuel Whitbread in 1795. John became the fifth Viscount for just one year. One of his original diaries is the treasured possession of the Luton Central Reference Library.

John Dunstable (died 1453)

A minor English composer and mathematician, John is believed to have been born in Dunstable. It has been said that 'he invented the art of musical composition', an undoubted overstatement. His work was better appreci-

The execution of Admiral John Byng on the quarterdeck of the Monarque.

ated on the continent than in Britain. His music was exclusively for the church and probably included the beautiful 'O rosa bella'.

John Howard (1726-90)

John Howard was born in Hackney, London, the son of an upholsterer. His parents died while he was still a boy. Using money left him by his father, he travelled abroad, and in 1756, while on his way to Lisbon, he was captured by a French privateer. He was taken to Brest prison, where he spent six dreadful days which made a lasting impression on him. Returning to a farmhouse at Cardington, left to him by his grandparents, he married Henrietta Leeds in 1758. Together they rebuilt the house, which can still be seen today by the church. With his cousin Samuel Whitbread he helped build a new parish workhouse and cottages for the villagers. In 1765 Henrietta died after giving birth to their son, John. Following a breach in the Independent church at Bedford, a New Meeting was set up, mainly at Howard's expense. In 1773 he became High Sheriff of Bedfordshire and inspected the local jail, discovering that prisoners were often unjustly detained without trial because they could not pay certain fees to their jailers. Consequently he visited many British jails to see conditions for himself. As a result of his efforts two bills were passed by Parliament in 1774 authorising county rates to be used for paying jailers a fixed salary and insisting on prison cleanliness. In 1777 he published his great work *The State of the Prisons*, which made him the foremost authority on the subject. In the following year he visited prisons all over Europe and Britain, noting reforms as they happened. At Kherson in the Ukraine he caught camp fever and died on 20th January 1790. On his Russian tomb are engraved the words: 'Whosoever thou art, thou standest at the grave of thy friend.' In England he is commemorated by statues in St Paul's Cathedral and the market square, Bedford. His name lives on in the Howard League for Penal Reform.

Dorothy Osborne (1627-95)

Dorothy was the youngest of the eleven children of Sir Peter Osborne, who during the Civil War held Castle Cornet as Governor of Guernsey for Charles I. When Dorothy was twenty-one she fell in love with William Temple, aged twenty. Temple was to achieve fame as a diplomatist and essay writer. For three years while Dorothy lived at Chicksands Priory they corresponded. His letters were lost, but hers survived and are considered some of the most delightful letters of the

Sir Joseph Paxton.

seventeenth century in the English language. They were married in 1665. When she died, thirty years later, she was buried with one of her children in Westminster Abbey.

Sir Joseph Paxton (1801-65)

The son of a poor farmer, Joseph Paxton became a major English gardener and archi-

tect. He was born at Milton Bryan and received little formal education. He became head gardener to the Duke of Devonshire at Chiswick and Chatsworth. Later he planned the gardens of Battlesden House in Bedford-shire. In 1850 he submitted designs for the Crystal Palace, which was built in Hyde Park, London, before being moved to Sydenham, where it remained until destroyed by fire in 1936. There is a memorial window to him in Milton Bryan church.

Thomas Tompion (1639-1713)

Thomas Tompion was born at Ickwell in 1639, the son of a blacksmith, also called Thomas. The son worked with his father until he was twenty-five years old, at which time he moved to London and became apprenticed to a watchmaker. In 1672 he began work as a journeyman clockmaker. Two years later he had his own business in Fleet Street, where he made and sold clocks and watches of all descriptions. In 1671 he was introduced to Robert Hooke, the inventor, and secretary of the Royal Society. In 1674 Hooke showed Tompion his designs for a spring-balance watch, and Thomas produced it. Tompion was soon recognised as the finest clock and watchmaker in London, and he produced watches for Charles II, James II and William III. In 1704 he was elected Master of the Clockmakers Company. Examples of his clocks are in Buckingham Palace, Hampton Court, the Fitzwilliam Museum at Cambridge and the Cecil Higgins Museum in Bedford. In 1982 the British Museum bought his finest clock, the Mostyn Tompion, for £500,000. Tompion died on 20th November 1713 and is buried in Westminster Abbey. There is a memorial plaque in Northill church.

Samuel Whitbread (first) (1720-96)

In 1734 the widow of Henry Whitbread sent her young son from Cardington to London to be apprenticed to a brewer. In 1742 he opened up a small brewery in Old Street in London, and eight years later he founded the Whitbread Brewery in Chiswell Street. He was married in 1758, and his son William (second) was born in 1764. His Bedfordshire home was The Barns at Fenlake near Cardington, and he became Member of Parliament for Bedford from 1768 until 1790, during which time he was one of Pitt's staunchest supporters. He was soon one of the wealthiest men in England and bought Southill House from the Torringtons in 1795, leaving it for his son to enjoy. He is buried at Cardington.

Samuel Whitbread (second) (1764-1815)

Samuel was born of nonconformist parents at Cardington. At the age of eleven he went to Eton, then briefly to Oxford and Cambridge, before making a Grand Tour in 1783 and marrying Lady Elizabeth Grey in 1788. Since 1785 he had worked in the family brewery in London. In 1790 he took over his father's seat as the Whig member of Parliament for Bedford, a position he held until his death in 1815. Inheriting Southill House, he had it modernised by Henry Holland. He enjoyed the country life and spent vast sums of money improving the houses and facilities of his tenants at Southill, Cardington and the neighbouring villages. He had a burning desire to help the poor, sick and uneducated. He enquired into the state of the county's workhouses and got them improved. As a magistrate he set up a 'justice room' at Southill where anyone could come to seek his help or advice. With John Howard's help he influenced the design of the new Bedford jail (1801) and later the Bedford Infirmary (1803), Asylum (1812) and new river bridge (1813). He was a great friend of John, sixth Duke of Bedford, and together as politicians and landowners they dominated Bedfordshire affairs. Whitbread was also a patron of the arts, building up a fine collection of paintings at Southill. He also helped the dramatist R. B. Sheridan rebuild Drury Lane Theatre after the fire of 1803. He committed suicide in London in 1815 and is buried with his wife Elizabeth in Cardington church.

10
Customs and events

Bedford Regatta. For information contact Bedford Rowing Club. Telephone: 01234 353183.

Usually held over the first weekend in July, all kinds of rowing events take place on the Great Ouse and can be easily observed from either bank.

Bedford River Festival. For information contact the Bedford Tourist Information Office. Telephone: 01234 215226.

Usually held every two years on the May Bank Holiday, this is an exciting day of water sports and activities providing entertainment for all the family.

Ickwell May Day celebrations. For information contact the Bedford Tourist Information Office. Telephone: 01234 215226.

The village has a permanent maypole on the village green around which the local children dance on May Day, nowadays on the May Bank Holiday.

Leighton Buzzard Beating the Bounds. For information contact the Vicarage. Telephone: 01525 373217. Held on Rogation Monday (May).

In 1633 Edward Wilkes built the almshouses for ten widows in North Street. His son Matthew endowed these in 1692. The choir marches from the church of All Saints to the almshouses, and while extracts from Matthew's will are read a choirboy stands upon his head outside the houses, 'the better to impress him'!

Pavenham Hay Ceremony. For information contact the Vicar. Telephone: 01234 720234. Held on 10th July.

Listening for the witch on Shrove Tuesday, on Conger Hill, Toddington.

In the past Trinity College, Cambridge (holders of the advowson), allowed the parish clerk to gather as much grass as he could cut in Town Field between sunrise and sunset during hay time. On 10th July, eleven days after the Feast of St Peter, the floor of the church is still strewn with new-mown hay in thanks for the first hay harvest. Perhaps the green man carving on the wall of the north aisle had a part to play at one time.

Riseley Good Friday Cakes. For information contact the Vicar. Telephone: 01234 708234.

Small cakes were to be distributed on Good Friday 'for ever' and made from wheat grown

Beating the Bounds outside the Wilkes Almshouses, Leighton Buzzard.

on Cakebread Close. Today hot cross buns are distributed instead.

Shefford Fair. Held on 11th October every year.

Originally this was called a horse fair, but it consists only of amusements nowadays. The right to hold a fair in Shefford was granted in 1312.

Toddington Shrove Tuesday ceremony

Just before midday on Shrove Tuesday (February or March) village children gathered on Conger Hill (page 60), the Norman motte behind the church. They lay with their ears to the ground as the church clock struck midday and they heard a witch frying her pancakes. The origin of the ceremony is unknown and has now almost died out.

Derelict Thurleigh mill with St Peter's church beyond.

11
Further reading

A wealth of Bedfordshire history, geography and natural history is to be found in the twenty-four volumes of *The Bedfordshire Magazine* published continuously since 1947. Most towns and villages have their own histories, which have proliferated so rapidly in recent years that it would be invidious to mention all but the most detailed. *A Bedfordshire Bibliography* by L. R. Conisbee (Bedfordshire Historical Record Society, 1962, with three supplements in 1967, 1971 and 1978) is invaluable for material published up to 1976.

Benson, Nigel C. *Dunstable in Detail*. The Book Castle, 1986.

Bigmore, Peter. *The Bedfordshire and Huntingdonshire Landscape*. Hodder & Stoughton, 1979.

Bunker, Stephen, *et al. The Changing Face of Luton*. The Book Castle, 1993.

Dony, J.G. *A History of the Straw Hat Industry*. Gibbs, Bamforth & Co, 1942.

Dony, J.G. *Flora of Bedfordshire*. Luton Museum, 1953.

Dony, J.G., and Dony, C.M. *The Wild Flowers of Luton*. J. G. Dony, 1991.

Dyer, James, and Dony, J.G. *The Story of Luton*. White Crescent Press, 1975.

Godber, Joyce. *History of Bedfordshire 1066-1888*. Bedfordshire County Council, 1969.

Godber, Joyce. *The Story of Bedford*. White Crescent Press, 1978.

Houfe, Simon. *Through Visitors' Eyes: A Bedfordshire Anthology*. The Book Castle, 1990.

Matthews, C.L. *Ancient Dunstable*. Manshead Archaeological Society, 1989.

Meadows, Eric. *Pictorial Guide to Bedfordshire*. White Crescent Press, 1982.

Mee, Arthur (revised J. Godber). *The King's England: Bedfordshire and Huntingdonshire*. Hodder & Stoughton, 1973.

Nau, B.S., *et al. Bedfordshire Wildlife*. Castlemead Publications, 1987.

Pevsner, Nikolaus. *The Buildings of Bedfordshire, Huntingdon and Peterborough*. Penguin, 1968.

Pickford, Chris. *Bedfordshire Churches in the 19th Century: Part I, A-G*. Volume 73, Bedfordshire Historical Record Society, 1994.

Simco, Angela. *Survey of Bedfordshire: The Roman Period*. Bedfordshire County Council and Royal Commission on Historical Monuments, 1984.

Smith, Worthington. *Dunstable: Its History and Surroundings*. 1904; reprinted Bedfordshire County Library, 1980.

Summers, Dorothy. *The Great Ouse – A History of a River Navigation*. David & Charles, 1973.

Trodd, Paul, and Kramer, David. *The Birds of Bedfordshire*. Castlemead Publications, 1991.

Underwood, Andrew. *Ampthill – A Goodly Heritage*. Ampthill Parochial Church Council, 1976.

Victoria History of England: Bedfordshire. Three volumes and index. A. Constable, 1904, 1908, 1912, 1914.

Willis, R. V. *The Coming of a Town* (Leighton Buzzard and Linslade). White Crescent Press, 1984.

Wroot, Sarah (editor). *Your Guide to Nature Reserves in Bedfordshire and Cambridgeshire*. The Wildlife Trust: Bedfordshire and Cambridgeshire, 1993.

12
Tourist information centres

Ampthill: 12 Dunstable Street, Ampthill MK45 2JU. Telephone: 01525 402051 or 406464.
Bedford: 10 St Pauls Square, Bedford MK40 1SL. Telephone: 01234 215226.
Dunstable: The Library, Vernon Place, Dunstable LU5 4HA. Telephone: 01582 471012.
Luton: 65-7 Bute Street, Luton LU1 2EY. Telephone: 01582 401579.
Luton Airport (Information Centre). Telephone: 01582 405100.
Woburn: Woburn Heritage Centre, 9 Bedford Street, Woburn MK17 9QB. (Open seasonally only.)

Manor Farm gatehouse at Tilsworth.

Index

Page numbers in italic type refer to illustrations.